Reflections of a Setting Sun

Healing experiences around death

To Deanna

Best wishes

Michael Barbato

14.11.15

Life is beautiful –
thank you Ann
for making this my reality

Reflections of a Setting Sun

Healing experiences around death

MICHAEL BARBATO

National Library of Australia Cataloguing-in-Publication entry:

Barbato, Michael
Reflections of a Setting Sun: healing experiences around death.

1st edition 2009
2nd edition 2016

Includes bibliography
ISBN 978 0 646 51456 7

Deathbed hallucinations
Near-death experiences
Terminal care

133.9013

Cover photograph: Michael Barbato
Design (interior and cover): Ruth Barbato
Editor and proof reader: Ann Barbato

Printed on 70GSM classic by Griffin Press, Adelaide

Other publications by Michael Barbato:

Caring for the Dying McGraw-Hill (2002)
Caring for the Living and the Dying (2010)
Midwifing Death (2013)

Paper used in this book is natural and recyclable, and is made from wood grown in sustainable forests.

Acknowledgements

This book was spawned by the death of a young man almost 30 years ago. He opened my eyes to the mysteries that surround death, and to their healing potential. Until then, I was blinded by the glare of life-saving medicine and saw death only as the end of life. I thank him and all I have cared for – they have been my teachers.

To my original editor, Kath Kramer – thank you for your skills. Your honest and helpful comments ensured I did not wander too far from the facts. There are times when I may have strayed a little, but this was only to reveal what I believe to be true. Jeane Balcombe's proof reading of the first edition was a real blessing. It rescued me from many embarrassing mistakes and came at a time when I was struggling to find words. Thank you Jeane.

The second edition is more of a family affair. I thank my life-long partner, Ann, for her unwavering faith in me. Apart from the onerous task of editing and proof-reading, she and our eldest daughter Claire critiqued the original drafts. Our second daughter, Ruth, displays her exceptional talent in the layout and design. James and David have supported me with their ongoing encouragement and countless questions.

The author gratefully acknowledges permission to reproduce the following copyright material

A quotation from the book *Magnanimous Despair* by Grahame Jones, copyright 1998, reprinted with permission from Boombana Publications, Mount Nebo, Queensland.

The poem 'There's a Hole in my Sidewalk' from the book *Autobiography in Five Short Chapters* by Portia Nelson, copyright 1993, reprinted with permission from Beyond Words Publishing, Hillsboro, Oregon.

Contents

It happens sometimes that the Angel of Death,
when he comes for a soul, sees that he has come too soon,
that the man's term of life is not yet expired;
so he does not take the soul away ...
but leaves the man one of the innumerable pairs of eyes
with which his body is covered.
And then the man sees strange and new things,
more than other men see and more than he himself sees
with his natural eyes.

SHESTOV, LEV
In Job's Balances 1975 (p.5)

* *My thanks to Graeme Garrett, St Marks, Canberra, for drawing my attention to this passage.*

Introduction

We live life forward
but only understand it backward

SOREN KIERKEGAARD

Lead us into the darkness
that we may find what lies concealed

MICHAEL LEUNIG

Introduction to the second edition

Following the publication of *Reflections of a Setting Sun* in 2009, a number of recent findings have thrown new light on some topics that book highlighted, namely dreams, deathbed visions and the moment of death. These discoveries are so important, a second edition of *Reflections* has been published to keep pace with developments and to explore their significance in relation to the mysterious events that accompany death and dying. It is also an opportunity to update many of the original chapters with information gleaned from the latest death and dying literature and from my experience in talking to dying patients and grieving relatives.

Since my retirement from clinical practice in 2013 I have been engaged in research around the care people receive at the end of life and the efficacy of treatment used to ensure comfort during this crucial period. The research has made small but significant inroads into our understanding of *unconsciousness* that precedes death and will, I hope lead to better care of people at the end of life. Ann and I have also established a Midwifing Death Correspondence Course for those in the general community who wish to know more about the art of caring for someone who is dying.

For the many who sit in vigil with a dying relative or friend, the transition from life to death is both surreal and painful. It often leads some to question the meaning of a protracted death and whether it would be more humane to speed up the dying process. In palliative care there are practices implemented to ensure a patient's physical comfort at the end of life. We are less confident, however, of what is happening at the psycho-spiritual level especially when someone is unconscious. Virtually all the knowledge we have of this time comes from reports of intensive care patients who recover from a period of unconsciousness and talk of their experience of being in this limbo-like state.

You may wonder why it is necessary to delve into areas such as unconsciousness and near-to-death experiences like deathbed visions. The reason is simple. For many years Ann and I have been running information sessions and workshops on death and dying. People are hungry for knowledge on these topics. They are seeking answers to questions that have, in many instances haunted them for years. The questions usually relate to an experience that occurred when a friend or relative was dying and which led them to believe this person was delirious, tormented or in pain. Because their grief was often paralysing, they were unable to ask for answers at the time. Following the person's death, the memory of the incident did not fade and their need to find an answer remained. The relief that came when they heard a plausible explanation was greatly comforting. This has left me in no doubt of the importance of death literacy – giving individuals and the community the information they need to care for dying loved ones, to understand what is happening, to be prepared for unusual experiences and to dispel myths that surround death.

As with the first edition, this second edition highlights the importance and relevance of the dying process. Death is not the result of a series of medical events spiralling out of control, but is a profound human experience that envelops the person dying, family, friends and those who deliver care. Regarding death as a failure of treatment not only ignores this experience but also adds to suffering. The late Bede Griffiths, a Catholic monk who established an ashram in India and wrote widely on Eastern religion, said, 'The cause of suffering is that an individual does not see their place in the pattern of the whole and is therefore in conflict with it" (Griffiths 1980, p.51). *Reflections of a Setting Sun* does not deny or glorify death but acknowledges its significance.

My interest in the more esoteric aspects of death and dying goes back some 30 years. At the time I was caring for a young man named Ian who was dying of acute leukaemia. Ian had been unconscious for several days, but for reasons I did not then understand he awoke as his sister, who had just arrived from America, entered his room. He opened his eyes, gazed upon her, smiled, lapsed back into unconsciousness and died several hours later. Although I had been in medical practice for almost 15 years I had never encountered anything like this. Colleagues that I spoke to were equally mystified or, in some cases, dismissive. In my six years of medical training there had been no mention of the possibility of an unconscious patient suddenly waking up so close to death. While that was some time ago, I do not recall death being discussed as anything but the end of life. The human experience and the phenomena that may take place were never mentioned.

Some of the most valuable lessons I have learnt come from people as they approach death. They have not taught me what it is like to die, for that is something we can only know through direct experience. They have, however, shown me the value of life and how important it is to live life fully. Over the years I have also learnt something about the art of dying and how important it is for the dying person to control the process and to trust that family, friends and carers will be there, irrespective of what course their journey takes. When asked about her experiences in caring for the dying, Mother Teresa said, 'The dying need tender loving care, nothing more' (Kessler 1997, p.xviii).

This book is an account of the many mysterious events I have seen or been told about during my twenty five years in palliative care. It raises questions about life and death, including the most vexed of all: is there life after death? I have not set out to prove that which cannot be proven but only to alert you to the countless mysteries and potential gifts that accompany death.

The book starts with a detailed look at the nature and variety of deathbed visions. They are what interest me most and because of my work as a palliative care doctor I am much more familiar with them than with the more widely publicised 'near-death' experience. My fascination with deathbed visions and other phenomena around death is not so much academic as existential. I am interested in what they say about life and death, the lessons they have for us individually and collectively, and how we can best respond to these teachings.

The following two chapters deal with the near-death experience; the nature of the experience, the various situations in which it occurs and finally its cause. There is much we do not know about near-death experiences (this is also true of deathbed visions), particularly their cause. Chapter 3 looks at some of the theories that have been or are currently in vogue. The 'left brain' approach taken in this chapter contrasts sharply with the more personal tone that permeates the remainder of the book, but the science of near-to-death experiences cannot be ignored even though it has been powerless to explain such enigmas. Chapter 4 explores what I like to call 'mysteries' around the time of death. These are unusual experiences that the rational mind struggles to understand and may be inclined to reject. They involve the dying person and also those who grieve, and include such things as out-of-body experiences, dreams, intuition and after-death communication.

Chapter 5 is more practical and describes ways we can prepare for our own death or the death of another. It reviews the medical and holistic models of care and indicates how each has an important place in the care of someone who is dying. This chapter concludes by probing the enigmatic state of mind called unconsciousness or coma. Chapter 6 confronts the final and greatest mystery of all. It explores the question of 'Who am I?' by outlining the journey of self-discovery that unfolds as the dying person peels back layers of personality, searching for what lies beneath. For many, this is a healing journey in which the dying person seeks and often finds meaning for their life and ultimately their death. The book concludes with the story of Aaron and his family. A remarkable story that highlights the sadness, confusion and complexity that surrounds death, and the powerfully healing messages that often surface despite (or because of) what is happening at that time.

All the stories come from real life. In some instances I was present at the time of the event but most were relayed to me by the experient or by a family member. Some have come from a distant relative or friend who knew of or was told about the experience, but was not present when it happened. These unsubstantiated accounts are in the minority but are included because of the valuable message they contain. Names have been changed and identifying features omitted to ensure anonymity. Permission to include stories was obtained whenever possible.

I have avoided the regular use of acronyms and medical terminology, even though many are in everyday use and would be familiar to most readers. The only term that requires some explanation is 'near-to-death experiences'. This is used as a matter of convenience to include any or all the experiences described throughout the book, including near-death experiences, deathbed visions, out-of-body experiences, after-death communication, feelings of peace and joy, significant dreams, et cetera.

The title for this book, *Reflections of a Setting Sun*, came from a conversation I had with an elderly Chinese woman who was dying of cancer. Although she spoke little English, Mrs. T and I were able to communicate using her children as interpreters. She told me about her faith, her culture and her beliefs, all of which were comforting to her at that time. When the subject of deathbed visions arose she became animated and not only indicated her belief in them but she also referred to an old Chinese saying that could be interpreted as, 'the last shining of a dying candle' or 'the transient reviving of the dying'. She did not like either expression and preferred her own metaphorical interpretation, 'reflections of a setting sun'. She wanted me to remember this and asked her daughter to record the saying on paper for me to keep. Mrs. T died at home with her husband and children by her side. Her words have lived on in my mind and the paper on which these words were recorded has survived and is reproduced below.

回光反照

Chapter 1

The nature and variety of deathbed visions

What we figure out in our head
looks quite different once realised in reality

PETER NOLL
In the Face of Death

Chapter 1

The nature and variety of deathbed visions

Profound mystical experiences are surprisingly common among those who are dying or those confronting a life-threatening situation. The near-death experience is undoubtedly the best known and most frequently reported of all the near-to-death experiences. The vivid and almost unbelievable accounts given by those who survive a life-threatening situation have stirred people's imagination and challenged the inquiring mind of scientists, philosophers and theologians. Visions experienced by the dying, commonly referred to as deathbed visions, are equally remarkable and no less frequent than near-death experiences. However, for reasons soon to be outlined, they hardly rate a mention in the medical or popular press even though a landmark book on the subject, written by Sir William Barrett, was published almost 50 years before Raymond Moody drew the world's attention to the near-death experience.

Sir William Barrett was professor of Physics at the Royal Academy of Sciences in Dublin from 1873 to 1910. Although steeped in science he had a long-standing interest in things that could best be described as paranormal. He was instrumental in establishing the Society for Psychical Research in Britain in 1882 and later became its president. His interest in deathbed visions was inspired by his wife, an obstetrician, after she told him about a vision, described to her in great detail by one of her dying patients. He was so moved by what he heard that he embarked upon a mission, and over several years uncovered stories of many deathbed experiences which he recorded in a book entitled *Death-Bed Visions*. While the book is still regarded as the first serious publication on the subject, doubt has been cast over the validity of some of the secondhand reports given by clergy and members of the Psychical Society, whose motivation and objectivity have been questioned. Despite this criticism, the book remains a landmark text; albeit a forgotten one.

Moody's book, *Life After Life*, first published in 1975, details the mystical experiences of more than 100 people who survived a life-threatening situation. The publication led to an immediate explosion of interest in near-death experiences that has continued to this day. Although the experiences described in Moody's book are no more remarkable than those described by Barrett, the popularity of *Life After Life* has, ironically, contributed to deathbed visions becoming a neglected, if not forgotten, subject. People wanted to know more about those who survived death than those who succumbed to it. Telling these stories, often via the popular press, generated enormous interest and in so doing it raised the profile of the near-death experience to the point where it is now part of our culture and our vocabulary. Deathbed visions on the other hand have, until recent times, been misinterpreted as a hallucination caused by medication, particularly morphine. The patients who spoke of their experience were often sedated and their story died with them. Only in recent times has the true nature and frequency of deathbed visions been fully appreciated.

Although discounted by many in the contemporary Western world, deathbed visions have been recognised throughout the centuries among a wide variety of cultures, including Indigenous people. They have always regarded them as 'heralding the onset of dying' (Kellehear 2007, p.82). Prior to my retirement I spent several years working in Central and Northern Australia. When the subject of visions came up, Aboriginal health workers and traditional healers stated that visions of pre-deceased relatives or 'spirits' are common among their people when they are 'finishing up'. The people in the vision come to lead the dying person to 'the other side'. Visions are accepted as part of the 'finishing up' process and surviving family members are not at all shocked or perturbed by what they are told or witness. They are, however, reluctant to share the experience with non-Aboriginal people, fearing something so significant will be misunderstood, dismissed or medicated. The visions are respected and honoured by Aboriginal people and, apart from being predictive of death they constitute an integral part of their 'Dreaming'. The vision alerts significant family members to the need to make the prescribed preparations for 'finishing up'; preparations that are not only unique to their culture but also to the dying person and his/her mob.

Despite the frequently described imagery of predeceased relatives, deathbed visions cannot be considered as proof of life after death. For many who have such an experience, however, the fear of death seemingly melts away and is replaced by an overwhelming sense of peace and love. This capacity to so radically transform the experience of dying is what makes the deathbed vision a moving and significant event in the life of a dying person and worthy of our recognition. The reluctance of medical journals to acknowledge a deathbed vision as anything but a hallucination is also changing. Their acceptance is a welcome change from just twenty years ago when reports of deathbed experiences were dismissed by some prestigious journals as too far removed from mainstream medicine to warrant publication.

Terminology:

The term *deathbed* suggests that visions experienced by those who are dying only occur at or around the moment of death. In a study of more than four hundred subjects who experienced a deathbed vision, Drs. Karlis Osis and Erlendur Haraldsson found that 12 per cent of the visions occurred within minutes of a person's death. The vast majority manifested hours, days or even weeks beforehand (1977, p.64). In a similar but smaller study, 50 per cent of deathbed visions took place within 24 hours of death and 38 per cent manifested more than one week before (Barbato et al. 1999).

So, while a significant number of visions occur when death is imminent, many take place well before, increasing the likelihood of them being mislabeled as hallucinations.

A similar issue arises with the word *vision.* Imagery is certainly the most common feature of a deathbed vision but auditory, tactile and olfactory experiences are not unusual. Anecdotal evidence suggests that hearing and touch are the last of the senses to be affected by the dying process, so it comes as no surprise to learn that auditory and tactile sensations can accompany the deathbed experience. Barrett devotes a whole chapter to music heard by the dying in his book *Death-Bed Visions*. In a more recent study, auditory features were described by 20 per cent of people who had experienced a deathbed vision (Houran and Lange 1997).

One explanation for the relative absence of sounds or words in deathbed visions may be found by examining dreams that occur during rapid eye movement (REM) sleep. We are more likely to remember REM dreams. Unlike 'thought' dreams which occur during slow wave sleep, REM dreams are replete with sensations, including vision, sound, smell and taste, as well as any number of emotions (Jouvet 1999). When a REM dream is recalled, what we most easily remember is the visual component and the emotional accompaniments. There may be some memory of what was heard and said but recall for the auditory component is typically distant or vague. The same is true for smell and taste, but even more so. Recent evidence suggests there may be a relationship between deathbed visions and dreams. If that is the case, it is not surprising that the emotional and visual content of a deathbed vision is remembered, often at the expense of all else.

The erroneous assumptions that result from the term *deathbed vision* have led to numerous other descriptors being used. These include End-of-life Experience, Nearing-Death-Experience, Nearing-Death Awareness, Deathbed Communication, Near-to-Death Experience and Death-Related Sensory Experience. While these are more precise in what they attempt to describe, it's unlikely that any will replace the time-honoured, but less-accurate *deathbed vision.*

The core features of a deathbed vision

One or more of the following features are commonly found with a deathbed vision:

- vision of a pre-deceased relative(s). Occasionally it may be a deceased friend, an unfamiliar figure, a religious identity, or a scene
- gesturing
- an ensuing state of peace and acceptance.

A vision of a pre-deceased person, usually a spouse, parent, sibling or relative, occurs in up to 70 per cent of all deathbed experiences. Visions of religious figures are much less common, accounting for just 13 per cent in those of Caucasian descent. When religious figures are seen, they are always integral to the person's belief system. Christians claim to see Jesus, Mary or angelic beings while Hindus see one or more of their gods (Osis and Haraldsson 1977, pp.65, 235). Other images such as scenes, trains and boats, are fewer in number. As with dream imagery, any deathbed vision has symbolic significance for the dying person and they readily associate it with a journey they are about to undertake. (Sanders 2007, pp.24–35).

> *Marcia had been unwell for many years. She had severe heart disease that confined her to bed for the last few months of her life. She was beautifully cared for by her loving daughter but found the gradual loss of independence to be almost intolerable. As she was dying, she said to her daughter, 'I want to go home...look at that beautiful yellow bird flying...I want to fly...I want to go home.'*

The dying almost always take comfort from this form of imagery. The same cannot be said of the family. They are usually frightened by what they see or hear and, more often than not, believe their relative to be hallucinating. This has unfortunate consequences. They recoil, and a golden opportunity for both to share something meaningful is lost forever.

If, for example the vision includes a train, the family could use this imagery at a later stage to guide their loved one, particularly during the unconscious phase that precedes death. The family could then say, 'Your train is at the station. We are sad to see you go, but we understand it is now time for you to leave.' Such symbolic language is readily understood by the dying person and its appropriate and timely use is a loving and gentle way of helping a dying person navigate the final moments of their life. You do not, of course, have to rely only on deathbed imagery to guide you in your choice of a metaphor. If the individual has been a keen sportsperson you might say, 'You have run a great race; you are now on the final lap and the finishing line is within sight'. Symbolic or metaphorical language is powerful and evocative. The art resides in choosing an aspect of your loved-one's life that is meaningful to them.

Irrespective of how and why they arise, visions of pre-deceased relatives, religious figures, heavenly scenes or symbolic images do, in the majority of instances, bring acceptance, peace and even joy to the dying person. Laura's story illustrates how an intuitive knowing of being greeted by a loved one at the moment of death can bring a degree of serenity that many of us would find unbelievable.

> *Laura had been unwell for many months. She had an aggressive form of cancer that had spread throughout her body. Laura was a determined woman and despite increasing weakness and weight loss she tenaciously hung onto her independence. It took a fall at home before she would accept admission to the nearby palliative care unit. Over time her condition deteriorated and it became clear to her family and carers that she was dying. Laura knew about her cancer but, as had been her habit, she politely steered any conversation away from her illness. She was frightened and her fear of death had been exacerbated by the sudden and unexpected death of her husband, Tony, some weeks before. The family and hospital staff wondered how she would cope when the moment of truth arrived. The night before Laura died she said to her daughter, 'Tony is coming tonight.' Stunned by this statement her*

daughter asked, 'What are you going to do?' to which Laura happily replied, 'I think we will go dancing.' Laura and Tony both loved dancing and it was at a dance that they had first met. Laura died peacefully, in her sleep that very night.

Whether a relation, friend, an unknown identity or a religious figure, most visions are not threatening and are often described by the dying person as welcoming (Wills-Brandon 2000). This is reflected in the type of gestures a dying person is sometimes seen to make. They may, for example, reach out or attempt to embrace whomever it is they see. If, as Ethier (2005) has suggested, the purpose of the apparition is to guide the person through the dying process, the gesturing may also reflect a willingness to follow. The thought of a messenger guiding someone during their final journey may sound fanciful, but Trent's story lends some credence to Ethier's suggestion.

Trent was a young man burdened by pain from a very aggressive cancer. Despite radiotherapy and large doses of morphine, the pain persisted necessitating his admission to hospital. Even though he was having large doses of morphine Trent remained lucid at all times. He was a popular personality and his hospital room was always overflowing with visitors. One evening, his father joined the hordes of people in the room and, as he went to sit on the only empty chair, his son called out, 'Be careful Dad; don't sit on my friend.' The father, looking at the empty chair asked, 'What friend?' Trent replied, 'He is a good friend and is here to help me', and then explained that this person had been with him for several days and often occupied a chair when one was available.

It is very easy to imagine how deathbed visions, particularly those that involve unrecognisable figures or confusing images, are labelled as hallucinations. This error is more likely to be made when the dying person is known to have a psychiatric history or dementia. In these situations, it is important to consider the possibility of a deathbed vision before attributing unusual imagery or behaviour to a medical or psychiatric cause. Elisabeth Kübler-Ross, the author of many books on death and dying believed that most of the dying, regardless of their mental status, have deathbed visions. The experience may be bizarre or impossible to communicate, but changes in behaviour can be revealing, as the following example illustrates.

Sally had been a resident of a dementia unit for almost 10 years. During this time she rarely smiled and was often aggressive. This behaviour persisted and indeed worsened as her physical condition deteriorated. Two weeks before her death the family noticed a sudden change in her behaviour. Instead of the agitated, unhappy person they had known for the past 10 years she was peaceful, always smiling, and sought to touch or stroke those who came to visit. She died in this loving space, a space that had been foreign to her until those final two weeks.

The idea that one can be peaceful around the time of death is something most of us would find hard to believe. Yet, a state of equanimity and acceptance is common among those who have a deathbed vision, including people like Sally who have dementia. A feeling of serenity is often verbalised, with many saying they no longer fear death. In others, it is their composure that suggests something has changed. It may be difficult to appreciate how anyone could be unafraid of death but the following words, uttered by a young mother as she lay dying immediately after the birth of her one and only child, gives us cause for hope: 'I can't stay – I can't stay: if you could see what I see you would understand' (Barrett 1986, p.12).

Children and deathbed visions

Few studies have looked at deathbed visions in children but anecdotal reports suggest they too see pre-deceased relatives and that these visions, like those of their adult counterparts, are comforting and affirming (Barrett 1986, Morse 1994, Ethier 2005).

> *Several years ago I was one of several doctors looking after a 5-year-old girl, named Neva, who had leukaemia. She had been sick for most of her short life and at the time of my involvement she was close to death. Although she was unable to express her feelings she was clearly frightened and for this reason had, for the past few months, shared her parent's king-sized bed at night. Every morning her father would rise early to make his*

> *wife a cup of tea. Neva was usually asleep at these times. One morning he was surprised to find her wide awake but chose not to say anything as her eyes were fixated on something outside of the window and, for the first time in many months, she appeared serene and peaceful. When he returned some minutes later, he found his daughter had died. It may be speculative, but I would like to believe Neva was not looking aimlessly out the window, but was captivated by a deathbed vision.*

Kübler-Ross often spoke of her work with children who were dying from injuries sustained in motor vehicle accidents that had claimed the lives of other family members. Although the children had not been told of the deaths, they frequently described visions of the family members that had been killed and at other times could sense their 'presence' about them (Kübler-Ross 1991, p.53). Elisabeth Kübler-Ross is often quoted as saying, "No one dies alone.' While there is no proof of this, the possibility is comforting, especially for grieving parents.

Children not infrequently describe visions of angels or angelic messengers and, as you would expect, these are perceived as comforting presences (Morse 1994, p.19). In her book, *A Window to Heaven*, paediatric oncologist Dr. Diane Komp describes many beautiful anecdotes involving dying children. These not only speak of a child's profound innate wisdom but also highlights their wonderful use of symbolism (1992).

An 8-year-old boy dying of cancer, whose parents had avoided talking to him about death, told them one day that he dreamed that Jesus had pulled up to his house in a big yellow bus and invited him aboard, telling him he was to die soon.

Unlike their adult counterparts, children also have visions of living relatives, teachers and even pets. Although present day reports of deathbed visions rarely include living beings, Barrett reported numerous instances of children, as well as adults, having visions of people who were alive at the time (Barrett 1986, pp.81-95). In most cases this involved what he called 'travelling clairvoyance' where the dying person was seemingly transported to another place where they saw the living person. This is more in keeping with an out-of-body experience, which will be described in more detail in a later Chapter.

The classic deathbed experience

The most striking of all visions are those that occur moments before death. I will never forget the first time I witnessed such an event. It occurred as I was nearing the end of a routine ward round. Many of the people I had seen that day had been admitted for treatment of troublesome symptoms but there were some, like Hazel, who were dying.

I entered Hazel's room wondering when her weary body would surrender to the mysterious unknown. She had been unconscious and unresponsive all the previous day and I had expected she would die that night. I was surprised to see she was still alive, but after many years as a palliative care doctor I have come to realise death's arrival is as unpredictable as death is unknowable. Some people die rather suddenly and much sooner than anticipated while others hover between life and death for days.

Hazel appeared peaceful. Her head rested on a single pillow, her eyes were closed and her fragile body was covered by a spotlessly clean sheet. Death was very near. Anne, her daughter and only living relative, had been called and was expected to arrive within minutes.

After a respectful check of her barely palpable pulse I stood in silence contemplating that unfathomable moment when someone crosses the line that separates life from death. Just as I turned to leave, Hazel sat bolt upright in the bed. I was amazed. Lazarus-like she had woken and for some inexplicable reason I thought she was about to ask a question. Her eyes, however, were fixed directly ahead. I spun around thinking her daughter must have entered the room but no one was there. I turned back to Hazel and asked, 'What is it?' But, there was no response.

Something had brought Hazel to life and captured her attention. Something that was invisible to me and the nurse with me. I asked, 'What can you see?' Again there was no response. I placed myself in her line of sight and repeated the question. Hazel looked straight ahead, engrossed and captivated by whatever she could see. Realising that I had intruded into hallowed territory, I stepped back and respectfully waited for what was to unfold.

Anne entered the room, baulked and turned to me for a reassuring explanation. With a minimum of words I indicated that her mother was having a deathbed vision and beckoned her to sit quietly by her side. Not unlike a child silently watching a favourite television programme, Hazel was consumed by whatever it was she could see and did not react to her daughter's arrival. Several minutes later she eased back on to her pillow and without a word or a sigh let go of life.

Experiences, similar to that of Hazel's are found in many of Barrett's publications (1918, 1986) but the following account attributed to Miss Frances Power Cobbe (Barrett 1986, p.4) is perhaps the most graphic depiction of the classic deathbed experience.

"The person is lying quietly, when suddenly, in the very act of expiring, he looks up – sometimes starts up in bed – and gazes on (what appears to be) vacancy, with an expression of astonishment, sometimes developing instantly into joy, and sometimes cut short in the first emotion of solemn wonder and awe. If the dying man were to see some utterly-unexpected but instantly-recognised vision, causing him a great surprise, or rapturous joy, his

face could not better reveal the fact. The very instant this phenomenon occurs death is actually taking place, and the eyes glaze even while they gaze at the unknown sight".

The sudden and unexpected eye opening, and gesturing as if to embrace someone are not uncommon in the classic deathbed experience and give us reason to believe thc dying person is indeed looking at something or someone. Whatever or whoever it is clearly brings them joy. For others who witness such a scene, the experience often invokes a completely different response. Shock and disbelief are the most common reactions. From the standpoint of a doctor, to have someone 'waken' just before they die is as incomprehensible as it is incredible.

The following story is taken verbatim from a recording with Kübler-Ross during a visit to Australia approximately 30 years ago and also appears in her 1991 publication, *On Life after Death* (1991, pp.53-55). This cameo provides a valuable insight into what transpires during a typical deathbed experience and highlights the overarching mystery that surrounds death and dying.

An American Indian woman who was knocked down by a hit-and-run driver on a highway was near death when a stranger stopped and asked if he could help her. She said, 'No, there is nothing else you can do for me. But, on second thoughts,' she said, 'if one day you go to the Indian reservation tell my mother that I was okay; that I was not only okay but very happy because I am already with my dad.' And then, she died in the arms of the stranger. This man was so touched that he was at the right time in the right place (sic) that he drove 700 miles out of his way to the Indian reservation where the American Indian mother told him that her husband, the victim's dad, died one hour before the car accident of a coronary on the Indian reservation 700 miles apart (sic).

The distressing deathbed experience

In their landmark multicultural study, Osis and Haraldsson reported numerous visions that were frightening or distressing to those who were dying. These visions occurred in 29 per cent of their subjects and for most, this negative response was not related to what they saw but to how they interpreted the experience. Most of them associated the imagery with impending death and were overcome with fear and anxiety. These responses were seen more commonly among people from the Indian sub-continent and when asked if they wished to accompany the apparition, one in three said they preferred not, while all but one person from an American sample said they were more than willing to go. This cultural difference is quite remarkable and while there was no obvious explanation the authors believe it is unrelated to religion or belief in an afterlife.

Very few of my patients, the majority of whom were Caucasian, described visions that were distressing. Family, on the other hand were disturbed by what they saw or heard and were often overcome by fear. This reaction contrasts with the positive response seen in the majority of experients at the time of their vision. It is possible that the family's response to what they see or hear reflects their underlying grief. A grief that is compounded by the shock of witnessing something they do not understand and were not expecting.

The hellish deathbed experience

The hellish experience is a vision that is truly frightening to the dying person because of its actual content. Fortunately, such experiences are a rarity. Barrett makes no mention of them, but in their survey, Osis and Haraldsson found seven per cent of all deathbed visions were threatening, with demons or devils recorded in almost half of them (1977, pp.238, 235). I have witnessed only one hellish deathbed vision in my 25 years of palliative care (see below).

Hellish visions may not, however, be as rare as the facts suggest. Many may be mistaken for a hallucination. Rather than demonic or hellish figures, the vision can be of bizarre images or patterns that make no sense, and for this reason are considered to be disturbing as well as threatening. The important message is that these visions often have an underlying meaning which, if unmasked, changes the outwardly hellish experience in to one that is comforting and healing (Fox 2003, p.346). The following true account is taken from my earlier book, *Caring for the Living and the Dying* (2010, pp.139-141).

> *Rhonda had been in the hospice for some time as we attempted to ease the pain and vomiting associated with her long-standing cancer of the bowel. I visited her*

late one morning and was pleased to hear the pain had improved and that she had not vomited in the previous 24 hours. A short time later, as I sat in my office, the nurse entered and informed me that Rhonda was greatly distressed. Her groans could be heard outside the room. I entered to find her writhing in pain and clutching a heat pack to her stomach. I asked, 'Tell me what is happening?' Much to my surprise Rhonda did not talk of pain but rambled on about a maze of red, brown and orange colours that clearly frightened her. As she spoke her face contorted and, drawing up her legs, she tightly held a heat pack to her stomach.

After some time, I asked if there was any place within this maze of colours where she could escape. 'Yes,' she replied, 'the dark blue is beautiful.' I was not sure what this signified, but every time the maze of painful and frightening colours appeared I asked her to return to the blue and, lo and behold, with this her pain and distress miraculously vanished, albeit temporarily. After some time I asked, 'Is there anyone there with you?' and to my surprise she said yes, and then identified an aunt and one other relative, both of whom had died some time before. I asked, 'Do they have a message for you?' to which she replied, 'Yes, it's okay.' And with this Rhonda relaxed, went to sleep and had no further pain. She died some 12 days later.

If a hellish vision is mistaken for and treated as a hallucination, the negative emotions associated with it may linger and the memory of that experience will continue to bother the dying person. Medical intervention with sedatives or psychotropic drugs will not alter this. Distinguishing a hellish deathbed vision from a hallucination is no easy matter. If confronted by this dilemma it is helpful to acknowledge that this may not be a hallucination. Invite the person to talk about their experience. An open question like the one I put to Rhonda, 'Tell me what is happening?' may bring a response that is both unexpected and revealing.

The following example attributed to Ram Dass (original source unknown) shows how acknowledging and validating the experience, irrespective of how bizarre it may be, can achieve more than conventional comfort measures that often includes sedation.

> *Staff members of a palliative care unit were at their wits end. An elderly man close to death had been making loud bizarre noises for several days. The staff had tried every nursing procedure to ensure his comfort, but to no avail. Believing him to be distressed by hallucinations they finally resorted to medication, but again without success. By this time other patients, as well as the staff, were concerned not only for the man but for their own sanity. In desperation they called Ram Dass, who regularly volunteered his services to the unit when they needed someone to sit with a dying patient. On this occasion they asked if he could work some magic and ease the man's distress.*

As Ram Dass sat beside the patient he was drawn to mimic the exact noise made by the elderly man. The staff was now most concerned as they had not one, but two people making loud noises. After a short time the man, who had not said an intelligible word for days, turned to Ram Dass and said, 'You can see them too', and with that he stopped making the noise and remained peaceful until his death some time later.

This and Rhonda's story offer an alternative approach to conventional medical treatment when faced with someone who is troubled by what appears to be a hallucination. Recognising the possibility of a deathbed vision is the most important first step. What happens next depends very much on the situation. In the absence of danger to the patient or others it is wise to proceed slowly and allow the situation to unfold. This holistic approach is likely to have a better outcome and is more respectful than one that involves an immediate pharmacological intervention.

What is not so clear is why an experience such as Rhonda's can change so suddenly into one that is positive and affirming. The highly respected transpersonal psychologist, Ken Wilber offers a possible explanation when he suggests all experiences of consciousness are interconnected and that any painful experience can suddenly transform into one that is joyful and meaningful (1983). He calls this sudden and dramatic shift in the way we experience things as the 'slingshot effect'. While this shift is thought to occur spontaneously it may, as in Rhonda's case, require someone to guide the process.

An interesting observation from studies of near-death experiences is that hellish encounters are no more common in those who attempt suicide or with victims of violence or trauma. More than 100 years ago the Swiss geologist and mountain climber Albert Heim collected many first-hand accounts of near-death experiences from climbers who had, like himself, survived a near-fatal fall. Contrary to expectations they all described comforting if not beautiful experiences that included a merciful, painless loss of consciousness at the moment of impact (Roberts and Owen 1988). If this is true of near-death experiences, it may also be true of deathbed visions.

How common are deathbed visions?

The exact number of people who have a vision at or around the time of their death is uncertain. Most estimates are based on the number of experiences recounted by those dying or witnessed by family and carers. Because many pass unnoticed or are misdiagnosed, assessments based on observations alone are likely to represent the tip of the iceberg. It is reasonable to assume that the incidence of deathbed visions increases as death approaches, and that loss of consciousness or sheer fatigue preclude these visions being shared or acted out. A recent study now suggests that visions occur in almost 90 percent of those who are dying (Kerr 2014). This is in keeping with the prophetic statement, 'No one dies alone' made by Kübler-Ross many years earlier. She believed visions of pre-deceased relatives are the norm rather than the exception.

Even when a person is capable and willing to share their experience, its nature and significance may be lost on others, particularly if the imagery is confusing or if family and friends have not been alerted to such possibilities. The family may then interpret the words and gestures as the ramblings of someone close to death and seek medical help in the form of sedation, believing this to be the kindest thing to do. Many profound visions may be overlooked in this way. The following example, taken from *Caring for the Living and the Dying* (Barbato 2010, p.138), illustrates this most clearly.

> *Nina was an elderly Italian matriarch. She had been admitted to the local hospice because of symptoms from advanced cancer. She was extremely weak and spoke very little English. She made no demands on her family or on those who cared for her. The family had requested that Nina not be told she was dying even though her body language suggested she already knew. Nina was close to death and the family was in constant attendance. One day Nina's daughter rushed from her mother's room, grabbed me as I passed by and pleaded that I give her mother an injection to settle her. She said her mother was agitated and was asking to leave the hospice. When I entered the room, Nina was sitting upright in bed, gesticulating and speaking in her native tongue. Her eyes were fixed straight ahead as though she was looking at something. What struck me was the smile that lit up her face. I turned and asked the daughter to interpret what Nina was saying...*

"My bags are packed, my boat has come, I am going on a beautiful holiday and none of you can come with me" is what she interpreted. Although Nina was overflowing with joy, the family was convinced that she was delirious. I explained it was not a hallucination but a deathbed vision and Nina was telling them in the gentlest and kindest way that she knew she was dying and that she was not afraid. Nina died two days later but not before she and her family said their good-byes and shared many beautiful moments.

Nina's joyful pronouncement is one of the most impressive examples of how metaphor or symbolism can simply and beautifully express that which is otherwise hard, if not impossible, to communicate. Metaphor is the linguistic tool that allows us to speak the unspeakable and comprehend the incomprehensible. It is the language a dying person automatically engages in when they need to communicate something of great importance. Unless we are fully attuned and aware, messages like Nina's fall on deaf ears.

A patient once asked a friend and colleague, 'How long before I die?' He had asked the same question of many others beforehand but had not received an answer that made any sense to him. Knowing his patient was a punch drunk boxer, the doctor resorted to the type of symbolic language he thought his patient would best understand. He replied, "The bell has sounded for the last round." The boxer immediately knew what the doctor was saying and never again repeated the question. The head does not hear [comprehend] until the heart has listened! (James Stephens).

Sharing and hearing a deathbed vision

If they have the strength, the dying may wish to share their experience. They will do this with anyone who cares to listen. In the context of a hospital or hospice this is frequently a nurse (O'Connor 2003) or a volunteer. Others may keep the experience to themselves, concerned that sharing could alarm relatives and add to their grief. Dying patients lock away much of what is important to them, often for this very reason. These may be memories, painful and confusing emotions, or deeply moving events such as a deathbed vision. For this reason family, friends and carers are encouraged to listen attentively to everything that is said and to avoid jumping to conclusions or putting their own interpretation on things that are unclear. 'Tell me more' or, 'What does this mean for you?' are good ways of opening up the conversation. If they are unusually quiet or distracted, you may then ask 'Is there something you want to share?' All that is then required is to listen carefully. Opinions or explanations are rarely sought. What they appreciate most is the opportunity to share what is on their mind or in their heart. This is their gift to us and our undivided attention is our gift to them.

Vision, hallucination or a dream

When a patient shares their vision, the immediate reaction of family, friends and some healthcare staff is that the person must be hallucinating because of the medication they are taking or from the ravages of the underlying illness. This is rarely the case. The imagery associated with a deathbed vision and those that result from a medical, drug-induced or psychiatric illness are clearly different and provide ample evidence to support the belief that there must be another cause. The major differences are as follows:

1. A deathbed vision is usually of a pre-deceased relative who the dying person recognises immediately. If the imagery is of some other person or place it is always clear and never distorted whereas that which occurs with psychosis or delirium is almost always bizarre and confusing.
2. Hallucinations associated with psychosis and those that have a pharmacological origin are usually accompanied by other psychological features such as confusion, unpredictability, behavioural changes and loss of awareness of normal surroundings (Stevenson 1983; Nayani and David 1996). These characteristics are rarely if ever seen amongst those who have a deathbed vision, except for the few who describe a hellish experience.
3. While the previous two differences are noteworthy, what clearly distinguishes a deathbed vision from a hallucination is the person's emotional response to what they see. Joy, peace and tranquility are part and parcel of a deathbed vision, but terror or alarm is the standard response to a hallucination (Gauntlett-Gilbert and Kuipers 2003).

Doctor Ian Stevenson, a psychiatrist with a long-standing interest in paranormal phenomena, says a hallucination is 'a waking sensory experience that has no identified external physical stimulus' (1983, p.1610). In other words, an individual sees and senses things that others cannot perceive. The deathbed experience certainly satisfies this definition. The content, context and emotional responses, however, are very different from a hallucination associated with a psychiatric illness or a medically-induced delirium. Stevenson is so convinced of the difference that he suggests the word *hallucination* should not be used when describing a deathbed vision to ensure they are not tainted by the stigma that goes with the word because of its association with mental illness.

Could a deathbed vision be a medication-induced delirium? For reasons already given this is most unlikely; a conclusion that is supported by the fact that deathbed visions occur with people who are on no medication. There have also been instances where patients have a typical deathbed vision and bizarre hallucinations around the same time. Not surprisingly, the hallucinations, but not the deathbed visions cease after the person's medication is changed or the dose reduced.

If not a hallucination, what then is the most likely explanation for these mysterious yet comforting visions described by those at the edge of death? Before elaborating, it is timely to remind readers that knowledge of the cause may satisfy our curiosity, but is of little interest to those who have a deathbed vision. The meaning they attach to the experience is what really matters as is the equanimity and peaceful state of mind that follows.

The most plausible theory to date is that a deathbed vision is an intense dream, so powerful and moving that it often wakes the dying person from their slumber and is consequently experienced as real (Kerr 2014; Grant 2014). In a study of 66 patients admitted to a hospice, almost all (88 per cent) described at least one dream or vision (Kerr 2014). A total of 267 dreams and visions were reported and of these most occurred when the subject was sleeping and a minority when in a 'wakeful' state. Unfortunately the wakeful state was not defined by the authors. If we assume it was more in keeping with daydreaming, then the occurrence of deathbed imagery during this so-called wakeful period is not unusual. Changes that occur within the brain during dreaming and daydreaming are very similar, the one major difference being that dreaming is a more intensified version of daydreaming (Fox 2013, p.412).

Half of the visions described by Kerr included deceased loved ones, while the remainder were of living friends, relatives, people, a meaningful past experience and, very occasionally, pets, animals or a combination of these images. All the visions were described as real and a sense of travel or moving on was apparent in 60 percent. This sense of reality underscores the intensity and emotional significance of the experience but it is also a consequence of an altered sense of meta-awareness; meaning the person is unaware they are dreaming or daydreaming (Schooler 2011). Perhaps the most significant and reassuring outcome of this and other studies (Brayne 2008; Lawrence 2012) is the observation that those who described a deathbed vision had a more peaceful death compared to those that did not. Kerr conclude by saying, "the emotional impact is so frequently positive, comforting and paradoxically life-affirming...the dreams/visions transcend the dying experience" (p.302).

The question that now begs an answer is whether the dream theory undermines the link that has often been made between deathbed visions and life after death (Barrett; Kübler-Ross;

Moody; Wills-Brandon). Even if deathbed visions turn out to be the product of life-like dreams, there is no proof that this is the complete story. At the time of a deathbed vision, Stafford Betty, Professor of Religious Studies at California State University says, 'we are witnessing the momentary merging of two worlds that at all other times remain tightly compartmentalised and mutually inaccessible' (one of these worlds is the real world, while the other could be the world of fantasy, dreams, delirium, the 'spirit' world or something beyond our comprehension). He concludes by stating that a critical but open mind is required when addressing this topic.

Chapter 2

The near-death experience

I saw more than I can tell and I understood more than I saw;
for I was seeing in a sacred manner
of all things in the spirit

THE NEAR-DEATH EXPERIENCE OF BLACK ELK
'Black Elk Speaks', in Bailey and Yates 1996, p.81

Chapter 2

The near-death experience

Raymond Moody's book *Life After Life*, published in 1975, may have drawn the world's attention to the near-death experience but stories of unusual events associated with life-threatening situations were not uncommon before then. Near-death experiences have occurred throughout the ages, with reports dating back two thousand years and involving people from a wide variety of cultures, religions and spiritual beliefs. Post-1975, however, there has been a flood of reports from people who, for any number of reasons, had until then kept their experiences to themselves. The advent of intensive care units and improved resuscitation techniques in the latter part of the last century contributed to this surge, with more people surviving life-threatening illnesses and going on to tell their story. This encouraged others to 'come out' with their experiences, which until then had been locked away for fear of ridicule or because they themselves did not understand or appreciate its significance. Others, like Black Elk, simply lacked the words to describe it.

Core features of the near-death experience

No two experiences are the same, nevertheless, a number of characteristic features have been described in association with the near-death experience (Bailey and Yates 1996, pp.5-6; Roberts and Owen 1988; Greyson and Stevenson 1980). The most frequently reported include:

- a sense of peace, joy and serenity
- an out-of-body experience
- a sensation of passing along a tunnel, seeing bright lights, hearing music, a life review, and visions of pre-deceased relatives or others
- ineffability
- a decision to return
- subsequent life changes.

It is rare for all these features to be present with the one experience, but when they are, the experience is referred to as 'quintessential' (Moody 1975; Ring 1980). The full-blown experience is easily identified, but the majority of near-death experiences have fewer features and occasionally pass unrecognised. The same is true of atypical experiences that have none of the core features and which masquerade as something totally different (Fox 2003).

There is some dispute over the minimum number of core features required before an experience is said to qualify as a genuine near-death experience. Some argue that a critical number must be present and that a sense of peace or joy on its own falls short of the mark (Ring 1980; Greyson 1983). While there are arguments to support this position, others take the view that any core feature occurring in the face of a life-threatening situation is exceptional and worthy of being called a near-death experience. Academics and researchers debate this, but what really matters in the long run is not the number of core features, but how the experience is perceived by the subject and the effect it has on his/her life.

Core features in detail

1. Feelings of joy, peace and serenity.

Irrespective of the circumstances, 50 to 60 per cent of all near-death experiences start with a feeling of peace, joy or serenity (Blackmore 1991, 1996). The fact they are not mentioned by some does not, of course, mean they are absent. Peace is more likely to be remembered if it is the central or only feature of a near-death experience, but is easily lost in the magnitude of a full-blown quintessential experience. It goes without saying this sense of serenity is usually absent in experiences that are perceived as hellish.

2. The out-of-body experience.

An out-of-body experience is reported by 75 per cent of people who have a near-death experience (Greyson and Stevenson 1980). This remarkable experience of feeling or seeing oneself outside the physical body is, however, not confined exclusively to the near-death situation. It can occur in other circumstances, provided the prerequisites of a peaceful mind and a relaxed body are met. Given that most near-death experiences occur in traumatic and life-threatening situations, it is hard to imagine those conditions being present at that time. It is, however, achievable.

When he was dying of throat cancer, the respected Indian mystic Ramakrishna said, 'While the external self may experience the ravaging effects of disease, the inner self to which we are most deeply connected, is totally at peace' (Blackman 1997, p.13). This ability to maintain a still mind and a relaxed body in the face of impending death may seem beyond the reach of most. There is, however, a well-known saying in palliative care – people die the way they lived. The likelihood of peace and serenity around the time of death is, therefore possible and more likely with those who have prioritised and practised this attitude throughout life.

The sense of being outside one's body may result in confusion and fear for the disembodied traveller. The realisation that they are out of and looking down on their mortal body may, at first, be confusing and unnerving. This initial response quickly gives way to complete acceptance and enormous compassion for their physical form, even though they sometimes find it hard to identify with the body and the situation they have left behind.

A review by Greyson and Stevenson in 1980 found that the majority of subjects who had an out-of-body experience were aware of a 'non-physical' body. They described it as lighter in weight but of the same size and age as their 'earthly' body, and sometimes without the physical burdens associated with their past or present illnesses. Over the years, claims have been made about the absence of pre-existing infirmities within this 'non-physical' form. This includes instances of blind people being able to see and stroke patients having the ability to walk without a limp.

Speaking about her clinical experience, Elisabeth Kübler–Ross says, 'We have questioned several totally blind people who were able to share with us their near-death experience. They not only told us who came into the room first and who worked on the resuscitation, but also the minute details of the attire and the clothing worn by the people present' (Martin 1990, p.164). Sounds extraordinary, but I was reminded of how little we know when one of my patients who suffered constant pain and who was unable to talk wrote a note to say that he was pain free and able to communicate normally during his out-of-body experience.

Many attempts have been made to verify the veracity of the out-of-body experience by placing hidden codes in hospital units, such as coronary and intensive care units, where near-death experiences are most likely to occur. These codes can only be seen by looking down from the ceiling and are invisible to those lying in a bed. Only once has this code been correctly identified, but circumstantial evidence suggests the subject did not have an out-of-body experience but climbed out of bed to look (Blackmore 2003, pp.358-359).

In his book, *Proof of Heaven*, the neurosurgeon Eben Alexander cites research from the University of Virginia which he believes offers irrefutable evidence for the out-of-body phenomenon (2012, p.153). Based on this as well as his own near-death experience which he describes in great detail, he concludes, 'These phenomena are real, and we must try to understand their nature if we want to comprehend the reality of our existence.'

While researchers debate the truth of the matter, there are numerous anecdotal reports of people perceiving and remembering events while unconscious or clinically dead. One of these was reported by a coronary care nurse, verified by her colleagues and recorded in the highly respected medical journal, The Lancet (van Lommel et al. 2001, p.2041).

> *A 44-year old man was admitted to a coronary care unit. At the time of his arrival he was comatose and blue. His dentures were removed and resuscitation commenced. The nurse in question put the dentures onto the trolley that contained the drugs and resuscitation equipment. Resuscitation continued for 90 minutes and by this time he had a normal heartbeat and blood pressure but he remained comatose and required ongoing artificial ventilation. One week later, after he had emerged from his coma, the nurse met up with the patient again and upon seeing her he said, 'Oh, you know where my dentures are, you were there when I was brought into hospital and you*

took my dentures out of my mouth and put them onto that trolley. It had all these bottles on it and there was this sliding drawer underneath and that's where you put my teeth.' The nurse, stunned by the extent of his recall, went to the trolley and discovered the man's dentures just as he had described.

In a subsequent conversation the man described his out-of-body experience. He had seen himself lying in bed while the nurses and doctors were attempting to resuscitate him and how he was afraid they would stop trying to bring him back to life.

3. Tunnel effect, bright lights, music, voices, life review, visions of pre-deceased relatives.

A near-death experience may end quite dramatically when the person re-enters their body. They then experience all the pain and drama they had been spared while disembodied. The more fortunate will move into an intermediate phase which often includes some or all of the features mentioned immediately above. The degree to which any of these phenomena are experienced varies, but most people describe them as unusually vivid and affirming. Thought processes speed up, time stands still and a non-judgmental life review may occur – their life flashes before their eyes – (Greyson 1993). Less than 10 per cent feel they are embraced by the light or enter the light, but when this occurs it is usually associated with an overwhelming sense of joy, love and understanding (Ring 1980).

Children have different experiences and, as with deathbed visions, are more likely to see living friends, relatives, teachers and even pets. Their experiences are more 'concrete', lacking many of the cognitive, emotional and transcendental features reported by adults (Morse 1986).

4. Ineffability.

Irrespective of the number of core features present, most say their near-death experience was so profound that they lack the words to adequately describe it. No matter how bizarre it may seem to others, the experience for them is more real than life itself. It is so precious, many are reluctant to share their experience for fear it will be dismissed as mere fantasy or as a fabrication.

5. A decision to return.

At some stage a decision to return is made. Sometimes individuals are told this is not their time, but in most instances they choose to do so. While the desire to continue this blissful journey is strong, the decision to return is taken because of family concerns (this is especially true of mothers with young children) or when there is unfinished business to complete (Moody in Bailey and Yates 1996, p.34). It is not so much a reasoned decision but an intuitive knowing that this is the right thing to do. When the message to return is given by those they see in the vision, it is communicated 'telepathically' rather than by the spoken word. Once the decision is made, the person finds themselves back in their body, and the illness or drama that precipitated the experience quickly, and sometimes miraculously reaches a favourable conclusion: the person survives (Moorjani 2012).

Angela was a married woman and the mother of two young children. I was her doctor during the final weeks of her life and the following story was recounted to me by her husband when I called in to see him at his home the day after his wife had died.

> *Angela was 42 when she died of cancer. As a young girl she became desperately ill with septicaemia and was expected to die. Much to everyone's surprise she survived and life went on as usual. Several years later she told her elder sister that, as she lay unconscious in her hospital bed, there was an overwhelming sense of peace and during this time she heard a voice say she would survive this illness but would die at the age of 42.*

6. Life change.

The life change that often follows a near-death experience may be profound and enduring. In some cases it may be the only indication that a near-death experience has occurred.

Any serious illness or life-threatening trauma is a wake-up call, and it is not uncommon for the 'survivor' to make radical changes to their way of life. So the burning question is whether the change that follows a near-death experience is a consequence of fright or whether it is related to the nature of the experience. Kenneth Ring said, 'The real significance of the near-death experience may not be simply that it promotes spiritual growth as much as the kind of spiritual growth it promotes' (Ring 1984, p.144).

The change that follows a near-death experience is enduring and involves a person's attitudes, values and beliefs. The more profound the experience, the greater the change (Ring 1980). In essence people become less materialistic, more spiritually aware, more concerned for the welfare of others and the planet and more interested in psychic phenomena. They have a firm belief in life after death and are therefore unafraid or less afraid of death (Kennedy and Kanthamani 1995).

The shift is different following any life-threatening situation that is unaccompanied by a near-death experience. It tends to be more health and survival orientated. My first twenty years as a doctor were spent caring for those who had survived a heart attack. Most of these individuals made dramatic changes to their lifestyles. They gave up smoking, lost weight, changed their diet, took up exercise and adopted a less stressful lifestyle. This was not a spiritual awakening but a practical and calculated attempt to postpone death. In contrast to those who had a near-death experience, their motivation was not an acceptance of death but rather a fear of it.

Circumstances common to near-death experiences

As the name suggests, the near-death experience occurs in association with an illness or accident that is or is perceived to be life-threatening. The following list is far from complete but gives some idea of the range of settings in which a near-death experience may occur:

- serious illness including cardiac arrest, septicaemia ('blood poisoning') or severe blood loss;
- surgery;
- near drowning;
- motor vehicle accident;
- failed suicide;
- prolonged period of isolation or sensory deprivation.

Because they are within a coronary or intensive care unit where events can be monitored closely, the cardiac arrest group has been the focus of most of the near-death research. Many of the stories that emanate from these units are remarkable. Doctors and nurses who resuscitate these patients are so intrigued by what they see and hear that many decide to investigate the claims being made (Lawrence 1995, 1997; Parnia and Fenwick 2001, Parnia et al. 2002; van Lommel 2001, 2004; French 2005). Findings from these studies suggest that 10 to 12 per cent of cardiac arrest survivors have a typical near-death experience, with a smaller number having what one researcher describes as a 'superficial experience' (van Lommel 2001).

The iconic near-death experience is described by the now deceased actor, Peter Sellers. Speaking after his first cardiac arrest in 1964, he says, 'I felt myself leave my body. I just floated out of my physical form and I saw them cart my body away to the hospital. I went with it. I was not frightened or anything like that because I was fine; and it was my body that was in trouble… I looked around myself and saw an incredibly beautiful bright loving light above me. I wanted to go to that white light more than anything' (Bailey and Yates 1996, p.73).

Perhaps the 10 per cent who recall what happened to them do so because the experience is as real and remarkable as that of Peter Sellers. But what of the remaining 90 per cent who have no memory other than 'nothingness'. Following his cardiac arrest and successful resuscitation in 1990, the late Kerry Packer said, 'The good news is there is no devil. The bad news is there is no heaven.' Despite the research data and comments like that of Kerry Packer, near-death experiences may be more common than the figures suggest. An explanation for this discrepancy may be found by turning to the example of dreams.

We all dream, but few remember their dreams or even that they actually dreamt. The only dreams most of us recall are those that are 'earth-shattering', highly emotive or that occur close to the time of waking. Most remain dormant, but like those that are remembered, they still evoke emotions which often influence the way we feel over the ensuing days (Merikle 1998, p.11).

The unconscious, as well as the conscious mind, has a great influence on the way we feel throughout the day. There is persuasive evidence to indicate that information perceived unconsciously, 'can have effects over a period of time that is measured in hours and days' (Merikle 1998, p.6). This may stretch out to months if the information perceived is personally relevant or meaningful (p.16). The other important finding is that information perceived unconsciously leads to automatic responses over which we have no control, whereas information perceived consciously is available to guide us in our choice of actions (Merikle 1998, p. 11). How we perceive information when we are unconscious is far from clear, but the ramifications of this information are vast and beyond our conscious control.

Most of us are familiar with the experience of waking in the morning and feeling irritable or on top of the world for reasons that are anything but clear. The mood is not due to the way we slept or what side of the bed we alighted from; it is the result of dreams we are unable to recall. These dreams and their accompanying emotions are preserved in perfect detail within the brain, but are not easily retrieved (Penfield 1975). Because they occur when we are asleep (Vis a Vis unconscious), their influence is, as Merikle suggested, pervasive and beyond our control.

There is now evidence to suggest a deathbed vision is an intense dream that carries into wakefulness (Chapter 1). The same or a similar process could also be said of a near-death experience. If following a cardiac arrest or some other life-threatening situation a person changes their way of life and thinking, it seems reasonable to postulate that they may have had a near-death experience, but one that was not intense enough to be remembered. This belief is supported by the work of van Lommel et al., who suggested it is the degree of stimulation at the subcellular level that determines 'whether the experience reaches consciousness and is remembered' (2001, p.2044). This means a near-death experience is more likely to be remembered if it is profound. All other experiences may be stored at an unconscious level and, although not accessible, they still have significant effects.

One of the most perplexing findings from studies of near-death experiences in cardiac arrest survivors is that the experiences seem to occur not before or after the arrest but at the time of the arrest, when circulation and cerebral function is most severely compromised (Parnia et al. 2002). Information presented later in the book (Chapter 5) about changes in brain wave patterns at the moment of death may help explain why this is so.

On a more mundane level, there is no evidence to suggest near-death experiences are more frequent amongst men or women, in certain age groups or in those who have a strong faith or belief in an afterlife. Similarly, the psychological profile of those who have an experience is no different from that of those who do not. There is a suggestion, however, that people who are more open to the possibility of transcendent states and who engage in spiritual practices are more likely to have a near-death experience (Roberts and Owen 1988). If the earlier assertion that a near-death experience accompanies all life-threatening situations is correct, it is plausible that those who are open to transcendent experiences are more likely to remember them, just as those who are interested in dreams more easily recall them.

Frightening or hellish near-death experiences

The so-called frightening or hellish experience is relatively uncommon and, depending on how it is defined, its incidence ranges from one to 18 per cent (Ring 1984; Rawlings 1980). Although Moody himself made no mention of negative experiences in his book, there have been numerous reports detailing transitory feelings of confusion and uncertainty arising from visions that are truly frightening or nightmarish. These visions may include demonic figures or disturbing images.

Greyson and Bush studied 50 accounts of 'distressing' near-death experiences collected by the International Association for Near-Death Studies (IANDS) and identified three distinct types of experiences. The first is the typical near-death experience which is interpreted by the person as distressing. The second is the experience of 'nothingness' and the third, and least common, is that with hellish images or scenes (Greyson and Bush in Bailey and Yates 1996, pp.209-230). While all three are distressing, only the last two qualify as frightening or hellish as the first says more about the person's response than about the experience itself.

The reasons why some people have hellish experiences are not absolutely clear. Most religious and philosophic traditions suggest that the state of mind at the time of a person's death (or near-death) determines what they experience at and after death (Rinpoche 1992, pp.108, 185-186; Yogananda 1995, p.720). In the preface to *Death, Intermediate State and Rebirth in Tibetan Buddhism*, the Dalai Lama says, 'Those who die within a virtuous attitude have a sense of passing from darkness into light, are free from anxiety and see pleasant appearances' (Rinbochay and Hopkins 1979). This belief is reiterated beautifully and symbolically by Teilhard de Chardin who says, 'Those who spread their sails in the right way to the winds of the earth will always find themselves borne by a current towards the open sea' (de Chardin 1968). So, while we may not know what predisposes someone to a frightening or hellish near-death experience (or deathbed vision), one possible way of ensuring against them is to lead a good and righteous life.

In the previous chapter I referred to the so-called 'slingshot' effect. This term was originally used by the transpersonal psychologist Ken Wilber to explain the dramatic shifts in consciousness that can take place with an out-of-body experience (Wilber 1977, p.170). In this scenario a person may go from pain to peace and back to pain again depending on whether they are in or out of their body. This slingshot model offers a plausible explanation for how deathbed visions can suddenly switch from hellish to joyful or vice versa. The change can occur spontaneously or may require a skilled intermediary. If this is true for hellish deathbed visions, it may also be true for hellish near-death experiences (Berman 1996, p.96).

Some would suggest that there is no such thing as a hellish near-death experience but only nightmarish experiences that may occur as a person moves from their serene disembodied state to the drama that awaits them in body consciousness. The nightmarish experience in this case is real and it may be triggered by what is happening to their body. When the life-threatening situation is imagined rather than real, the nightmare is not constructed from what they are experiencing physically but from the machinations of their mind (Wilber 1983, pp.82-99). In either case, it is body consciousness that predisposes them to a hellish near-death experience and the out-of-body experience frees them from this nightmare.

Chapter 3

The cause of the near-death experience

An uncontrolled mind that is attracted to the world and tries to understand things through reasoning alone will always remain skeptical and in doubt.

JOHN DAVIDSON
The Gospel of Jesus

Chapter 3

The cause of the near-death experience

The causes put forward to explain the near-death experience are diverse, complex and confusing. Some believe near-death experiences, like deathbed visions, are evidence for life after death whereas others claim that the experience can be fully explained by changes in the brain's normal physiology. The drive to find the cause(s) is not surprising as we live in an era, where, as John Davidson suggests, we try to understand all things through reasoning alone and those that cannot be explained this way are viewed with scepticism and disbelief.

This raises the interesting question as to whether phenomena which defy logic such as the quantum world, certain states of consciousness and paranormal events are unknowable to the rational mind. They may, as some suggest, require new ways of knowing and an openness to mind-bending possibilities. Ross and Joshi, both eminent researchers in the field of paranormal experiences, say the goal of research is not to determine whether an experience is real, but to objectively analyse the data in the hope of discovering some of the more important pieces of the puzzle (1992, p.359). This is not as easy as it sounds for in trying to determine the cause of a near-death experience we are fundamentally dealing with the mystery of consciousness. What confronts researchers and philosophers is a profound dilemma which is highlighted by the following question, 'How is the water of the physical brain turned into the wine of consciousness?' (Humphrey 1992, p.210).

Before entering into the mine field of possible causes, the question that should be addressed is whether near-death experiences and deathbed visions are variations on the one theme, and if so, is there a common cause? While each involves an alteration in the experience of consciousness, the near-death and the deathbed experience are dealt with separately in most research publications as if to suggest they are different entities with different causes. The context for each experience is clearly different, but there are features common to both. Whether this means their causes are similar is yet to be determined. The possible cause of deathbed visions has already been discussed in Chapter 1 and what follows applies only to the near-death experience. So, while the remainder of this chapter probes the roots of a near-death experience, the fruits that spring from these origins should not be forgotten. They are, according to William James, 'a great deal more significant than their roots' (Berman 1996, p.166).

The transcendent theory

Ever desireless, one can see the mystery;
ever desiring, one sees only the manifestations,
And the mystery itself is the doorway
to all understanding.

LAO-TSU
Tao Te Ching

The transcendent theory proposes that there is a continuation of consciousness after death. While some adherents to this theory would prefer the use of the word 'life' rather than 'consciousness', the term, 'transcendent reality' mentioned by Peter and Elizabeth Fenwick in their book, *The Art of Dying* (2008, p.212) is one that should satisfy both factions. While ever desiring, the possibility of life after death cannot be proven (or disproven), but the following story recorded by Kübler-Ross (1991, p.32) makes one wonder how and from where such information is accessed?

> *A young boy who had just recovered from a serious illness could hardly wait to tell his mother he had met his brother while he was ill. He had no doubt at all about the truth of this even though he had no brothers in real life. His mother was alarmed as the only brother he had was one who died many years before his birth and, for reasons best known to the parents, the boy had never been told about his sibling.*

If you think the Church is a strong supporter of the transcendent theory, think again. The theological response to this debate can best be described as cautious and intellectual, and is set out in great detail by Mark Fox in his excellent and appropriately named book, *Religion, Spirituality and the Near-Death Experience* (2003). The views expressed in this book suggest that the same degree of polarisation and confusion exists with clergy and theologians as with those in the secular world. The British theologians Linda and Paul Badham say, 'Reports made by resuscitated persons about their supposed observations provide some of the strongest grounds for supposing that the separation of the self from the body is possible' (Fox p.68). On the other hand Fox himself states, 'Twenty five years after the coining of the actual phrase 'near-death experience', it remains to be established beyond doubt that during such an experience anything actually leaves the body' (Fox p.340). The German scholar Hans Kung attempts to settle the matter by responding to his own rhetorical question, 'What then do these experiences of dying imply for life after death?' His answer is brief and uncompromising, 'To put it briefly, nothing' (Fox p.65).

Kung's conclusion is based on two concerns. Firstly, mystical experiences similar to those around death can occur spontaneously throughout life, as a result of drug use or brain surgery. If these experiences are not held up as evidence for 'immortality', he sees no reason why a near-death experience should be. His other objection is based on the fact that a near-death experience is associated with clinical but not actual or biological death. From this he concludes, 'Close as they were to the threshold of death, they never passed over it' (Fox p.65).

So where does this leave those who seek answers from theological scholars? Simply stated, we cannot expect authority figures, religious or secular, to resolve the conundrum of life after death. It is not something that can be proved or disproved, nor is it a concept that can be understood by the rational mind. According to one spiritual teacher, the quest is equivalent to an ant trying to comprehend the workings of the New York stock exchange. If true knowledge is experiential, we will have to wait until death to find the answer. Fox is a little more optimistic and concludes, 'The next quarter-century of near-death research may yet bring answers and closure to questions that remain, at present unanswered and tantalisingly open' (p.358).

What we are fundamentally dealing with is the mystery of consciousness and whether it survives death. Reductionists believe consciousness is a by-product of the brain and results from a combination of electrical, chemical and neuro-hormonal activity within dedicated and complex webs of neurones. If we believe this, we can only conclude that consciousness dies when the brain ceases to function and there can be no such thing as life after death unless you introduce abstractions like the soul or spirit.

Adherents to this form of reductionism accept that near-to-death and other 'mystical' experiences take place but that they arise from disturbances in brain activity. In other words, any near-to-death experience is a light show created by a brain that is dying or one that is threatened by the possibility of death. When that person dies, they say the lights then go off permanently. Recent studies have shown that the answer may not be so straight forward. Indeed, findings from these later studies suggest that the so-called light show may become brighter and more vivid at the moment of death. This raises the possibility of something more remarkable happening. This change and its possible significance is discussed under the heading, *The Moment of Death* in Chapter 5.

An alternative model to the reductionist theory has been proposed by the Buddhist physicist Dharmawardena (1996). He suggests that consciousness is not a property of the brain or a by-product of the brain's activity. He says it is a non-material entity, with an independent existence and remains within and interacts with the brain while there is life, but leaves the body temporarily with mystical experiences, when life is threatened and with impending death. The departure, he says, is permanent with biological death.

The literature on this subject of consciousness is enormous and complex and it is hard for someone of my limited knowledge to do it justice. For those who wish to read more, I recommend, the works of Ken Wilber, a transpersonal psychologist who has devoted a lifetime to the exploration of human consciousness. In addition, the mystics and the Eastern spiritual traditions offer experiential knowledge and concepts, as well as practices that can be followed around the time of death.

Neurological theories

Reason is incapable of grasping transcendent realities

KEN WILBER
Eye to Eye 1983, p.18

It is well known that chemical shifts within the brain can induce many of the features associated with a near-death experience. These shifts can be initiated by a life-threatening situation, but also occur with benign states such as migraine and epilepsy or with certain medications. Not surprisingly then, many consider a near-death experience to be nothing more than a chemically-induced hallucination. This view is prevalent within scientific circles, even though no single physiological change is regularly or consistently found in all near-to-death experiences, nor is any one change capable of inducing all the characteristic features of any experience (Fox 2003, p.342). Despite the inconsistencies it is important to at least mention some of these theories.

The scientific data on near-to-death experiences is vast, complex and beyond the scope of this book. I have limited myself to the most significant theories, which are presented in an abbreviated form. The references I have cited will, however, allow interested readers to pursue the subject more fully. Each hypothesis is discussed separately but it should be remembered that none occur in isolation and each is but a mere ripple in a tsunami of neurological change that occurs around the time of death or near-death.

Hypoxia

A reduction in the amount of oxygen reaching the brain (cerebral hypoxia) has been shown to induce many of the core phenomena associated with a near-death experience including the tunnel effect, a central bright light, movement, colours and memorable dreams. It does this by stimulating changes throughout the brain, especially in the visual cortex (Siegel 1980; Blackmore 2003, p.310).

Doctor James Whinnery (1990) reviewed 501 episodes of artificially-induced loss of consciousness in healthy volunteers.

Each subject was placed in a large centrifuge and exposed to increasing gravitational stress until loss of consciousness occurred as a result of cerebral hypoxia. The period of unconsciousness lasted almost 12 seconds and was followed by a recovery period during which many of the subjects reported tunnel vision, bright lights, an out-of-body experience, a feeling of euphoria and memorable dreams. The similarity between this and the near-death experience is self-evident, but the significance of the research is thrown into doubt by the fact that many who have a near-death experience are not hypoxic at the time (Parnia and Fenwick 2001).

Cerebral hypoxia can certainly induce many of the core features, but to say it is the cause of the near-death experience has yet to be substantiated. Proponents of the transcendent theory could argue that hypoxia, like many of the other causes yet to be discussed, simply frees the rational mind to experience higher realities.

Hallucinations secondary to medication or illness

It is now generally well-accepted that near-death experiences are not part of a delirium caused by medical illness or drug toxicity. Visual and auditory hallucinations are commonly associated with medical illness, psychosis and the use of certain medications including morphine. The imagery, however is invariably bizarre and frightening, and any human-like figures are generally unrecognisable (Gauntlett-Gilbert and Kuipers 2003).

In his book, *The Death of Forever*, Darryl Reanney tells the story of a person who, earlier in his life had a near-death experience and subsequently decided to compare that experience with the effect of taking a number of hallucinogenic drugs. He concluded, 'Whereas the drug-induced condition brought about sensory disorientation, the near-death experience was cogent, indelible and overwhelming; the effects of the drug-induced state faded quickly whereas the memory of the near-death experience remains…to this day' (1991, p.258).

Epileptic discharges within the temporal lobe of the brain

The classical 'grand mal' fit is characterised by sudden loss of consciousness, followed immediately by a stiffness of the body, violent shaking and frothing at the mouth. Unlike the former, a temporal lobe fit manifest in a myriad of ways that include lapses in consciousness, hallucinations, out-of-body, religious or mystical experiences, flashbacks, déjà vu phenomena, a life review or unexplained emotional swings.

As the name suggests, temporal lobe fits originate from within one or other of the temporal lobes and frequently arise because of some underlying brain pathology such as scarring, tumour or migraine (Austin 2006, pp.306-312). Because the temporal lobes are very sensitive to physiological change, the suggestion has been made that any of the circumstances that predispose to a near-death experience may be enough to evoke epileptic discharges, even in previously normal temporal lobes (Persinger 1983, 1999). The reported absence of characteristic epileptic activity on brain wave testing at the time of a near-death experience (Morse 1994, p.70) does not dissuade advocates of this theory. They believe the seizures may be so infinitesimal (microseizures) as to be missed on ordinary brain wave monitoring. Persinger says the physiological changes found around the time of death or near death 'should be' the strongest precipitants of temporal lobe seizures and that the mere anticipation of death may be enough to induce a microseizure (1983, p.1259).

Even if microseizures are shown to exist, this would not automatically establish a connection between them and any near-to-death experience. Professor VS Ramachandran, director of the Centre for Brain and Cognition and one of the world's leading brain researchers, suggested during an Australian radio interview that the temporal lobe may be, among other things, our antennae to the transcendent and the means by which the transcendent is made known to mankind. In other words, the temporal lobe may be the receiver rather than the originator of near-to-death and other mystical experiences.

Persinger's temporal lobe theory is far from convincing. Although many of the phenomena found with a near-death experience can arise from disturbances within one or either temporal lobe, visual imagery is specific to the occipital lobes. This undermines the theory, as does the clarity and consistency of the images perceived. It is hard to imagine the perfection and beauty of a near-death experience arising from the maelstrom and chaos normally associated with a seizure.

Endorphins

Endorphins are the body's own natural opioid (morphine-like substance) and are released at times of physical and emotional stress. Apart from preventing or easing pain they also induce feelings of well-being and joy (Blackmore 2003) and are responsible for the runner's 'high', a mystical-like feeling reported by many athletes.

Endorphins are not only released during times of pain but also with real or imagined life-threatening situations, and are thought to be responsible for the peace and ineffability commonly described with near-death or deathbed experiences. This link was made following a report of a near-death experience becoming hellish after an injection of a drug that blocks the action of endorphins (Judson and Wiltshaw 1983). So, while endorphins may contribute to the pain-free, ineffable aspects of a near-death experience, they play no role in the formation of images or sounds, which are core features of most experiences. At best they are minor players in the genesis of mystical experiences that occur around the time of death.

Psychedelic compounds

The list of drugs and naturally occurring compounds known to induce hallucinations is endless. Most drugs achieve this by interfering with neurotransmitters (naturally occurring chemicals within the brain) which facilitate the transmission of information from one nerve cell (neurone) to another until the message reaches its final destination. This transmission takes place in a rapid, orderly manner and may involve numerous neurones, neurotransmitters and their receptors.

There are countless neurotransmitters within the nervous system, particularly the central nervous system, and each is designed to carry one or more specific messages. Some are involved in the maintenance of consciousness, others with sleep, movement, pain, vision, hearing, taste, smell, the way we think and how we feel. In fact, everything that happens within the nervous system relies on one or more neurotransmitters. There are a host of drugs, chemicals and naturally occurring compounds (some formed within the brain) which are known to block or facilitate neurotransmission. These include glutamine, N.N-dimethyltryptsamine (DMT), Lysergic acid (LSD), ketamine (a drug occasionally used for pain relief or as an anaesthetic agent) and nitrous oxide (laughing gas). Some of these agents lead to phenomena that resemble or are characteristic of a near-death experience.

Doctor Karl Jansen, a psychiatrist with a long-standing interest in near-death experiences, believes compounds manufactured within the brain (including endorphins) may be responsible for many or all features of a near-death experience. His belief is based on research and personal experience. He admits to several near-death experiences and has also induced near-death experiences by self-administering ketamine. In contrast to the comment made by Darryl Reanney (reported earlier in this chapter), Jansen concluded, 'The near-death and ketamine experiences were clearly the same type of altered state of consciousness' (Jansen 1995, p.58).

This is a rapidly changing field of research which may ultimately give some clues as to the cause of the near-death experience. To cover it adequately is beyond the scope of this book and those who wish to read more are encouraged to find other credible sources.

The psychological theory

> *All our knowledge brings us nearer to our ignorance.*
>
> TS ELIOT
> *The Rock*

Many researchers, particularly those with a psychological background, attribute near-to-death experiences to a form of dissociation that protects individuals during life-threatening situations. Dissociation is a coping mechanism that psychologically healthy people resort to when their physical or psychological self is threatened (Ross and Joshi 1992). It has been described as, 'The separation of thoughts, feelings or experience from the normal stream of consciousness and memory' (Greyson 2000, p.460). Dissociation allows an individual to separate thought from fact. In the context of death, it permits the dying, 'To exclude this unpleasant reality from consciousness and replace it with pleasurable fantasies which protect them from being paralysed by emotional shock' (Roberts and Owen 1988, p.613).

The extent to which a person shuts out fear and panic depends on how well they can separate from the situation. While dissociation seeks to protect the psyche, a cascade of physiological changes unfolds to protect the body from perceived injury. The net effect is to isolate the person from the drama and trauma that envelops them. It effectively seals the person off from the outside world and in so doing it predisposes them to 'inner' experiences such as feelings of peace or joy, out-of-body experiences, comforting images and the sound of beautiful music. The greater the degree of dissociation the more profound the experience (Roberts and Owen 1988).

Impending death is perhaps the greatest of all threats, so it is not at all surprising that dissociation has been put forward as a possible explanation for the near-death experience. The account of near-fatal falls described earlier by Heim are good examples of dissociation in the face of death. In most instances the dissociation was more than a separation of mind from the body. It often included many of the inner experiences described earlier.

Dissociation is not only protective nor is it confined to near-to-death scenarios. It can arise during contemplative prayer, meditation, with childbirth or when totally absorbed by a beautiful scene, sunrise or sunset. These are often referred to as 'peak experiences'. In the poem 'Vacillation', the Irish poet and dramatist William Yeats vividly describes how this type of experience can unfold spontaneously (Finneran 1996, p. 249).

My fiftieth year has come and gone,
I sat, a solitary man,
In a crowded London shop,
An open book an empty cup
On the marble table top.
While on the shop and street I gazed
My body of a sudden glazed;
And twenty minutes, more or less,
It seemed, so great my happiness,
That I was blessed and could bless.

As a person moves more deeply into a 'peak experience' they become oblivious to all else around them. Indeed, as the verse above suggests, detachment from the 'thinking' mind is a pre-requisite for any peak experiences. During a Mind Science Forum with Australian scientists, the Dalai Lama stated, 'Subtle levels of mind cannot exist while grosser levels are operational' (2002). A peak experience can, therefore be thought of as a transition from body consciousness to higher consciousness. The experience of body consciousness is very much of this world and is influenced by the physical senses as well as the prevailing thoughts and emotions. Higher consciousness on the other hand dissociates us from these encumbrances and opens us to a range of mystical experiences that are otherwise unavailable. The distinction between body and higher consciousness is very clearly revealed in the following words of St. Paul, 'For our gifts of knowledge and of inspired messages are only partial; but when what is perfect comes, then what is partial will disappear' (1 Corinthians 13: 9-10).

Any near-to-death experiences may represent a transition into higher consciousness. The unresolved question, however, is whether this transition and the resulting experience take place because of changes within the brain (the neurological or psychological theories) or without (the transcendent theory) or from a combination of both.

Chapter 4

Mysteries around death

Death is not our shadow, it is our guide.

GURUMAYI CHIDVILASANANDA
Siddha Yoga Guru

Chapter 4

Mysteries around death

Dying is generally perceived as a painful and frightening experience. This is particularly true in contemporary Western society where death is not only thought of as a pall over existence but also as the enemy. Few see death as the spiritual teacher Gurumayi Chidvilasananda does, a guide for the way we live. For most it is a taboo subject that is deliberately or instinctively avoided, even when it stares us in the face. Death is too painful to contemplate, an attitude poignantly captured by Woody Allen when he said, 'It's not that I'm afraid of death, I just don't want to be there when it happens.'

No one wants to die, but death is inescapable. If we know this, why then do we give it so little thought and why do we not prepare for it? There are, of course, no glib answers, yet the questions are worthy of our exploration. The answer may reside in the idea that death is, for most of us, surreal and remote whereas life is real and immediate. Why should we concern ourselves with something so morbid and so removed when there is so much to live for? There are things to do, tasks to accomplish, goals to achieve, people to meet, places to visit, relationships to foster, love to give and receive, conflicts to resolve, knowledge to acquire, fun to have and so the list goes on. We are so busy living life we rarely stop to question its purpose and meaning. A culture [or an individual] that denies death is the biggest barrier to having the best possible death (Doughty 2014).

The unexamined life, said Socrates, is not worth living. It militates against a person living to their full potential. Such an existence neglects the fact that life is our best teacher. In failing to reflect upon its lessons, we risk repeating our mistakes until the negative consequences ultimately overwhelm us. As one of my dying patients said, 'It's not what I did that I regret; it's the things I didn't do'. He wasn't referring to personal goals he had not achieved but to intimate relationships he had taken for granted and broken fences he had failed to mend. Unfinished business had accumulated in this man's life and to his enormous regret he lacked the time and opportunity to remedy the things that were now important to him and which made his dying harder than it needed to be.

In her poem 'Autobiography in Five Short Chapters', Portia Nelson paints a picture that many will identify with (Nelson 1994):

I walk down the street. There is a deep hole in the sidewalk. I fall in. I am lost.... I am helpless. It isn't my fault. It takes forever to find a way out.

I walk down the same street. There is a deep hole in the sidewalk. I pretend I don't see it. I fall in again. I can't believe I am in this same place. But it isn't my fault. It still takes a long time to get out.

I walk down the same street. There is a deep hole in the sidewalk. I see it is there. I still fall in...it's a habit...but, my eyes are open. I know where I am. It is my fault. I get out immediately.

I walk down the same street. There is a deep hole in the sidewalk. I walk around it.

I walk down another street.

Do you regularly fall into holes, metaphorically speaking? Do you repeatedly make the same mistakes? Do you ever hear yourself saying, 'not again'? Would you live life differently if you knew you were going to die tomorrow? If you answer yes to any of these questions, why wait until you are dying to make changes? The gift of life is easier to surrender if we have made the most of it. That does not mean milking it for all it is worth but asking how much effort we have put into making the world a better place.

Commenting on those who die from cancer, John Paver says, 'It is my belief that people who have led a congruent and integrated life (no matter the details of their beliefs) will be able to face their cancer [hardships] and live courageously and creatively until their death' (2002, p.149).

Ironically, the fear and anxiety that surround death are, in no small measure due to the fact that we shy away from death and do not reflect upon it. In the words of the poet philosopher Rainer Maria Rilke, 'If the devils are driven away, the angels will also take flight.' Death is real and ever present. When we probe its mystery, we not only liberate ourselves from the fear of death but we also discover there are gifts to be had.

The need to prepare for death is beautifully illustrated in the following allegory, attributed to the Buddha, in which he compares the last thoughts of a dying person to a herd of cows in a barn. He says, 'When the barn door is opened, the strongest cow will go out first. If no cow is particularly strong, the habitual leader will go first. If no such cow exists, the one nearest to the door will go first. In the absence of any of these, all will try to get out at once' (Blackman 1997, p.16).

This chapter will not address a person's motives for acknowledging or shying away from the reality of death. It will however attempt to unwrap some of the mysteries that surround death, knowing that 'In gaining awareness of death we sharpen and intensify our awareness of life' (K and T Wilber 2001)

The out-of-body and the out-of-mind experience

> *The us that lives in our physical selves isn't limited by the skin and hair that defines our bodies*
>
> GREGG BRADEN
> *The Divine Matrix* 2007, p.10

The out-of-body experience has been defined as a separation of consciousness from the body or the ability to perceive the world from a location outside of the physical body (Blackmore 2003, p.356). It is most commonly described by those who have a near-death experience (Chapter 2) but can occur as a distinct entity devoid of the imagery and auditory component that accompany the former. Whether this out-of-body experience is an incomplete form of a near-death experience or a different phenomenon is unknown and probably unimportant. Suffice it to say there is a considerable overlap and sometimes it is hard to know which of the two is being described.

A typical description of an out-of-body experience is as follows: 'People find they are in a room detached from and often suspended above their physical body. The environment seems normal but brilliantly illuminated; hearing may seem more acute and mental processes sharp but detached. There is a sense the self is no longer occupying the physical body, but not that a second body is around the person' (Roberts and Owen 1988, p.608).

This extraordinary experience of consciousness leaving the body is said to occur in approximately 10 per cent of the general population, most commonly when sensory input from the outside world is reduced, as with deep relaxation, meditation or prayer (Blackmore 1984). The popularity of recreational drugs and hallucinogenic mushrooms is attributed to the out-of-body-like experience that frequently accompanies their use. Disease in an area of the brain concerned with self-processing (the temporo-parietal junction) can also result in disembodied experiences and this has led some to suggest that out-of-body experiences remote from a near-death situation may have an organic basis (Blanke et al. 2005).

Out-of-body experiences also occur during periods of prolonged isolation and sensory deprivation. In the context of a life-threatening situation, this is a potent mix and can predispose to delusions, visual and auditory hallucinations as well as the full-blown near-death experience. This was the case with Stuart Diver, the sole survivor of a large landslide that destroyed and buried many residences at Thredbo some years ago. Among the dead were his wife and many work colleagues. Amazingly, Stuart survived in freezing conditions for 65 hours during which he had many 'wild dreams' and frequent hallucinations of being rescued or of committing suicide. He also described a characteristic out-of-body experience, saying, 'It felt like my mind had moved to another level. Moved away so it could observe me from a distance' (Diver 1999, p.107).

The range of experiences described by Stuart Diver is a poignant reminder that consciousness exists, not as a single entity, but as a whole range of experiences. The American philosopher and psychologist William James was one of the first in the Western world to probe this and other mysteries bordering science and religion. He said, 'There are all about it [normal waking consciousness], parted from it by the filmiest of screens … potential forms of consciousness entirely different' (James 1985, p.388).

In those 65 hours underground Stuart Diver experienced normal waking consciousness, sleep consciousness, dream consciousness and disembodied consciousness in the form of an out-of-body experience. The partial separation of consciousness from the senses during sleep and dreaming became complete with his out-of-body experience. These experiences transported his mind from the emotional and physical pain associated with the tragic event and were, in a strange way, both life and mind saving.

People injured in a motor vehicle accident, or any accident for that matter, frequently report the absence of pain even though they may have incurred serious or extensive injuries. Near-drowning victims describe total detachment from their struggle and a sense of peace prior to losing consciousness. The near-drowning experience can be so profound for some survivors to say that drowning is a good way to die and that they no longer fear death.

I have vivid memories of my own near-drowning, even though it occurred 65 years ago. I was unable to swim but still managed to reach deep waters by holding on to a large rubber ball and drifting with the tide. Before I could bask in my feat the ball popped from my grasp and as it floated away, I sank beneath the surface. I remember going under several times and then, miraculously, the struggle ceased. I had no sense of being within my body and overwhelming panic was replaced by stillness and peace. Opening out before me was a panoramic view of the shore and the people there. Even though I was not aware of being out of my body, it was a perspective one could only get from well above the water line. I felt intimately connected to everyone I could see. I particularly remember a young couple walking hand in hand along the beach and at some intuitive level I knew they were on their honeymoon. I could sense the love they felt for each other. Although keenly aware of this, I had no awareness of the drowning body I had seemingly left behind. My next memory is of waking up, with my mother by my side. My elder brother had seen my predicament and came to the rescue, but not before the experience had already brought its own form of deliverance.

In 1892 the Swiss geologist and mountain climber Albert Heim recorded his own and other climbers' experiences of near-fatal falls as follows (Roberts and Owen 1988, p.607)

> *No grief was felt nor was there any paralyzing fright. There was no anxiety, no trace of despair or pain, but rather calm seriousness, profound acceptance and a dominant mental quickness. The relationship of events and their probable outcomes were viewed with objective clarity, no confusion entered at all. Time became greatly expanded. In most cases, consciousness was painlessly extinguished, usually at the moment of impact, which was at the most heard but never painfully felt.*

Recently, I received a phone call from a dear friend to tell me her son had died in a plane accident. Her grief was overwhelming and at the centre of her sorrow was the all-consuming fear that he suffered immense pain and anguish immediately before and at the moment of impact. Heim's observations paint a different picture and give us cause for hope. Based on his research, consciousness may exit the body before a potentially traumatic or life-threatening event reaches its climax.

There is now little doubt that out-of-body experiences occur during acute, life-threatening situations. But do they occur with protracted illnesses such as cancer, motor neurone disease, dementia and organ failure? Using deathbed visions as a guide, it is not unreasonable to assume that altered states of consciousness, including disembodied consciousness, occur within this group and that the frequency of all experiences increases as death nears. Roger Cole, a palliative care physician and spiritual teacher, says in his inspirational book *Mission of Love*, that as death approaches, the person gradually lets go of all worldly attachments and ultimately their own physical body (1999, pp.79-85). This gradual withdrawal from the outside world creates ideal conditions for out-of-body and other mystical experiences.

Several years ago I was asked to see a young woman named Sally. The diagnosis of motor neurone disease had been made several years before and at the time of my visit she was confined to a wheelchair. What troubled her most was extreme shortness of breath. Survival was only possible with the aid of a device that assisted her breathing. As her condition deteriorated she could not do without this machine for more than a few seconds at a time. She could whisper, but only by removing the mask for the briefest of time. Despite her perilous condition, her mind was sharp and she was fully aware right up to the moment of her death. Seconds before she died, Sally removed her mask and gazing into my eyes she whispered, just loud enough for me to hear, 'It's a strange feeling… my mind has left my body.' These were her last words and, while it is risky to speculate, I believe she was describing her very own out-of-body experience.

Out-of-body experiences are not unique to those who are dying. Several years ago a young woman came to see me after she had read of my interest in unusual experiences around the time of death. She wanted to tell me of an out-of-body experience that took place immediately prior to the birth of her first child. She had decided on a natural, drug-free birth and was admitted to hospital after her waters broke. Her husband was not present when she went into labour and fearing he would miss the birth she 'left her body' to see what was detaining him. The birth was uncomplicated except for the absence of the father. When he arrived some time later, he was suitably scolded by his wife who went on to describe exactly what he was doing in those minutes before the birth. He was shocked, for what she said to him was correct in every detail right down to a telephone conversation he had with a friend prior to setting off for the labour ward.

The thought of consciousness leaving the body may seem unlikely, but every night as we dream, our consciousness roams while our sleeping body remains parked within the bed. A young woman whose husband, Chris, had not long before died from a brain tumour wrote to me and said, 'As I was falling asleep one night with my baby next to me. I rose out of my body to the ceiling. Chris was next to me, just watching over us. Very peaceful.'

Our consciousness can also wander during times of meditation, contemplative prayer and even when we exercise. I call these out-of-mind experiences and consider them to be variants of or smaller versions of the out-of-body experience. Speak to someone who meditates regularly and they will tell you how they sometimes enter a state where time stands still, thoughts dissolve and there is no meta-awareness (awareness that they are aware). A dying person may have the same experience while daydreaming or during the transition between being awake and asleep. This experience is transient and the return to reality, though gentle, brings with it the discomfort and angst associated with their illness. If the experience is broken prematurely by a loud noise or by someone waking them from their sleep or musing, re-entry may be distressing and disorientating.

The palliative care physician, Michael Kearney suggests these temporary absences or out-of-mind experiences, "Contain, often in the most unlikely and darkest corners, and in the most unexpected disguises, exactly what is needed to deal with the particular question, challenge or life crisis that confronts us" (Kearney 1996, p.56). In their own subtle way these experiences, like all other near-to-death experiences are instruments of healing and every effort should be made to ensure they run their natural course and are not disrupted by noise or unnecessary interruptions.

Not so long ago most deaths occurred in the privacy of the home. Now, in Australia, 60 per cent of all deaths occur within hospitals and fewer than 20 per cent at home (Currow, Burns and Abernethy 2008). Rather than the peace and relative quiet of home, those dying in hospital are often exposed to excessive noise and endless activity. Some put up with this, particularly if their stay is brief. For others, particularly those who will never return home, the experience can be unpleasant with few opportunities to enjoy the peace and quiet they crave or the liberating out-of-mind experiences that may otherwise come their way.

Several years ago I attended a conference where two nurses presented a paper describing the care dying women received in their ward. Midway through the presentation a cacophony of sounds made it difficult to hear what was being said. Believing it to be thoughtlessness on the part of those in the audio-visual room the chairperson rose from his chair and addressed them saying, 'Please turn off that racket; we cannot hear what is being said.' The nurses approached the chairperson and explained that the racket was a recording of background noise in their ward that sick and dying patients had to endure on a daily basis. Such noise is not only an annoyance it is also the greatest impediment to an out-of-mind experience taking place.

Sadly, hospitals have become less of a treatment place for the sick and more a work place for the healthy. Noise, routines and distractions often mean there is little time for a patient to rest or sleep. Even if all is quiet, sleep does not come easily. A study of the sleeping pattern of patients in a surgical intensive care unit showed that all were severely sleep deprived. The sustained wakefulness was partly attributable to bodily discomfort and a noisy environment, but a fundamental change in the sleep-wake cycle secondary to illness was thought to be a contributing factor (Aurell and Elmqvist 1985). These conditions combine to create a hospital environment that is anything but therapeutic.

Dreams

What if you slept?
And what if, in your sleep, you dreamed?
And what if, in your dream, you went to heaven
And there plucked a strange and beautiful flower?
And what if, when you awoke,
you had that flower in your hand?

SAMUEL TAYLOR COLERIDGE (1772-1834)

The mystery of dreams is slowly unravelling. Research over the last 75 years has given us a good understanding of how they arise, but little idea of what determines their content. There is strong evidence to indicate that dreams arise from a unique combination of electrical and chemical activity in specific parts of the brain during sleep. The resulting images and accompanying language are colourful, bizarre and often defy interpretation. The following three dreams, however, go beyond our current understanding, stretch our imagination and defy belief.

> *Several years ago I cared for Albert, a young South American man who was dying from cancer. Immediately after his death, his wife rang close family members, including Albert's brother in Chile, to inform them of the death. 'I know,' was the brother's comment. 'Albert appeared to me in a dream several hours ago to say good-bye.'*
>
> *Margaret woke screaming one night. She dreamt her twin brother, who lived on the other side of the world and whom she had not seen for several years, was seriously ill. As it turned out, her brother had, at that very moment, sustained serious injuries as a result of a motor cycle accident.*
>
> *Josephine dreamt her father was calling for her. She woke and said to her husband, 'My father is dying', and without phoning to check if what she dreamt was true, she packed a bag and boarded the next train to Sydney, some 300 kilometers away. When she arrived, she found her father had been admitted to hospital the previous day with a diagnosis of leukaemia. When she entered her father's*

room he said, 'Oh Josephine I was praying that I might see you before I die.'

Sleep is a natural event. Its onset and offset is influenced by a number of factors including the body clock, while its quality and duration is dependent on environmental conditions and the person's emotional and physical health. It's a time when the body rests, recuperates and heals (Shapiro and Flanigan 1993). Sleep is composed of two distinct phases: rapid eye movement (REM) and non-rapid eye movement (non-REM) sleep. The former is characterised by vivid imagery and the latter by so-called thought dreams or no dreams at all. The two phases alternate and their relative duration depend on many factors, particularly the age and health of the person. Some parts of the brain are fully 'awake' during REM sleep while the body is totally relaxed to the point of paralysis. For healthy adults the average duration of each REM cycle is 20 minutes, with approximately 90 minutes between each cycle. Babies spend much more of their sleep time in the REM phase, but this diminishes as they move into their childhood years.

There is no end to the number of beliefs once held about the origin of dreams. It's not hard to imagine the awe and mystique these vivid nocturnal streams of thoughts, imagery and emotions must have held for earlier civilizations, and the power people attributed to them. While much of the magic has fallen victim to science and research, new data has emerged that, shines light on the healing potential of dreams and daydreams (Chapter 1).

The following are a few of the beliefs and superstitions once attributed to dreams:

- messages from the gods
- visits by demons
- messages from the soul, which is always awake and free to roam only while the person sleeps. In his book *The Paradox of Sleep*, Jouvet briefly describes customs and practices some tribes adopted to ensure the soul of the sleeping person is not disturbed and remains free (Jouvet 1999).
- a healing rite. The ancient Greek physicians believed illness could be healed when the soul came into contact with the divine through dreams. In Greek mythology, Asklepios, the god of medicine was worshiped in temples located in Athens, Kos and Epidaurus. The sick who sought healing went to these temples where, after a ritualistic preparation, they spent one or more nights sleeping in the temple. The remedies required to heal their ailments would then be revealed in their dreams. This healing ritual is described in great detail by Michael Kearney in his book *A Place of Healing* (2000, pp.66-82).
- an exploration of the 'otherworld' where the dreamer learns about death through encounters with the dead (Kellehear 2007, p.51). This belief was common among early hunter-gather communities and many Stone Age cave paintings are thought to depict some of these dream figures.
- a temporary psychosis
- a psychological safety valve that helps to maintain sanity
- an expression of repressed or unfulfilled wishes
- a prediction for the future that awaits.

Although science cannot explain 'the role of the mind in the machinations of the night' (Jouvet 1999, p.98), most scientists agree that the content of dreams, particularly those with a strong emotional overtone, is influenced by recent events in the life of the dreamer. Ann Faraday likens the dreaming mind to a movie director 'picking up things from waking life that need more attention…and reflecting on them in depth by composing stories' (Faraday 1974, p.4). This form of playback theatre consolidates memory and presents the dreamer with symbolism and metaphor for a real life situation that may have, until then, been ignored, repressed or denied.

Dreams are neatly locked away within the brain and more often than not are inaccessible to the conscious mind. If they have a strong emotional content they are more likely to be remembered and not infrequently recur until there is some form of resolution. The following story, taken from the book *Caring for the Living and the Dying* (Barbato 2010, p.277), illustrates this point.

> *Steve had been in the palliative care unit for some time and despite signs of impending death he maintained a brave face and refused to acknowledge or talk about the things that troubled him. He could not, however, hide from a recurrent dream of someone trying to slay him with a knife. This troubled him so much he ultimately talked about the dream and his fear of dying, and for the first time he started to cry. His dreaming mind had recognised that which needed attention and presented him with vivid symbolism that could not be ignored.*

Rarely are dreams about death so explicit. The dying commonly dream of boats, trains, falling, travelling or being trapped (Sanders 2007). These forms of symbolism, though more subtle than Steve's, are a potent force and often lead both the dying and their carers to confront reality. Dreams, said Freud, are the royal road to the unconscious. They can uncover fears that are too difficult for waking consciousness to contemplate (and which it therefore denies). Along a similar vein, Ann Faraday says, 'Dreams reflect a whole host of thoughts and feelings that passed us by during the day because we were too busy or unwilling to catch them' (Faraday 1974, p.4). Concerning the dreams of those facing death, Mary Ann Sanders says, 'The unconscious seems to be preparing the conscious for what is ahead' (2007, p.63). If true, it is ironic that we who care for the dying spend so much time probing their waking consciousness for answers while we rarely, if ever, consult the oracle of their dreams.

Mary had been caring for her sick husband, Mike, for some time and while his death was clearly inevitable she was unable to even contemplate the thought of his dying. One morning Mike awoke, and with a frenetic energy recounted to Mary a dream he had that previous night. In that dream he was sitting a university examination and was told the results would be made known in three days. He held Mary's hand tightly and said, 'Always remember this dream.' He was telling her what he knew and what she could not accept. Mike died three days later.

To dream about the death of a relative who is not sick says more about the dreamer's unconscious concern for them and, in the view of most dream analysts is rarely if ever predictive of what lies ahead. There are of course exceptions. Albert's appearance in his brother's dream may have been a measure of the brother's own fears and expectations, but could also represent an example of after-death communication (see later in this chapter).

The British biologist Rupert Sheldrake introduced the concept of morphic resonance as far back as 1981 to explain phenomena such as telepathic communication, synchronicity and the so-called hundredth monkey effect (2005). He suggests that individuals and groups establish morphic fields and the greater the similarity between the fields the greater the resonance between the individuals or groups. If true, it is reasonable to assume that resonance may be more powerful during sleep when much of the outside interference is excluded. If the relationship is strong and personal, as was the case with Albert, Margaret and Josephine, the connection is, according to Sheldrake, greatly magnified.

Gregg Braden has written widely on spirituality and science, and believes events such as synchronicity, déjà vu, the power of prayer and distant healing are more than random coincidences. He suggests, and refers to published research in eminent scientific journals to support his claim for the existence of a subtle energy field that not only links all of us but also every atom within the entire universe. He calls this power the *Divine Matrix* and suggests it is the medium through which we experience transcendent insights, as in dreams and through gut feelings or intuitive knowing (Braden 2007). The following example lends support to the 'mind-bending' theory of interconnectedness proposed by Braden and Sheldrake.

> *Joy was greatly distressed by her mother's illness and impending death. She sat holding her hand, not wanting to let it go for fear of 'losing' her. Early one morning tiredness got the better of her and at 2 am Joy returned home to catch up on sleep. She awoke at 6 am and recalled a vivid dream of rolling down a hillside and crashing into bushes. During the dream, she was frightened, but at some point the fear was supplanted by a profound sense of peace, something she had not felt since her mother was diagnosed with cancer. No sooner had she woken than she received a phone call from her father to tell her what she now already knew: her mother had died.*

Dreams frequently tell the living and the dying far more than they know or are prepared to acknowledge. In many instances they stretch understanding and break the shell of denial. In Chapter 1 we saw how dreams may, in those close to death, take the form of a deathbed vision that gently prepares the dying person for what awaits them. Dreams are windows into the unconscious and permit us to see much of what is hidden from our normal waking consciousness. They are, according to the ancient Greeks, a form of divine wisdom that can exert great influence. As with the ancient ritual of Asclepius, the symbolism and messages that accompany dreams and deathbed visions of today are potent sources of healing for the sick and dying. Dreams during times of crisis and transition illustrate the important role they play both in our living and our dying. We should honour them and the wisdom they accord by paying more attention to them.

Intuition

The intuitive mind is a sacred gift
and the rational mind a faithful servant.
We have created a society that honours the servant
and has forgotten the gift.

ALBERT EINSTEIN

The mind *knows* the world via the senses and through reasoning and reflection. What we see, hear, read, touch, smell or taste presents us with factual information which the mind shuffles through and then creates its own version of reality. The interpretation of any or all of this data is often biased because of embedded concepts and beliefs that have a cultural, religious or spiritual origin. As a result, the reality we figure out in our head is frequently distorted by what is already there.

The way we *experience* reality is, however, altogether different and comes through an innate wisdom we commonly call intuition. Intuition works independently of the intellect and because it is a 'no thought' state, it is less likely to be twisted by the mind. It is, according to one spiritual teacher, a mirror; 'It does not create anything, it only reflects that which is' (Osho 2001, p.60). Because it is a state of 'no thought', intuition – unlike reason – is not incompatible or uncomfortable with mystery. The intellect, says Osho, 'is involved with the known and the unknown, not the unknowable... intuition works with the unknowable – that which cannot be known' (Osho 2001, p.xi). Death and the idea of death is unknowable and explains why intuition can be so much more valuable than logic with those who are dying or who are overwhelmed by a spiritual or existential crisis.

Much has been written about reason and intuition. The former is a function of the left or dominant hemisphere while the latter is a feature of the right or non-dominant hemisphere. Both hemispheres, after the age of five years, work in tandem and together they give us a *stereoscopic* view of reality. The left is more concerned with detail – logical and analytical reasoning, sequential and temporal information processing – whereas the right accumulates socio-emotional nuances, and has a broader perception of the outside world (Joseph 1992). Much of what the right hemisphere intuits remains unconscious mainly because the left hemisphere is pre-occupied with taking in and analysing data. Despite this, the right hemisphere continues to receive and synthesise information while the left hemisphere is busy and also when we are asleep, unconscious or under a general anaesthetic. This information may lie dormant but often 'leads to automatic responses that cannot be controlled by the perceiver' – the so-called Freudian slip (Merikle 1998, p.11).

When we communicate with another person, the verbal message is always accompanied by a non-verbal component. The former is explicit and processed by the left hemisphere whereas the latter is perceived by the right hemisphere. Generally, the verbal message corresponds with the non-verbal cues that accompany it. When the verbal and non-verbal messages do not align, we are more inclined to believe the latter as we trust our innate interpretation of the event (*intuition*) more than the explicit details (*information*). Because the rational mind is so dominant, however, we do not always hear nor follow the still quiet voice within.

Children are particularly attuned to this form of 'unconscious' perception and are adept at reading between the lines. They are remarkably astute and pick up subtle nuances the communicators themselves may not be aware of. Some experts say this is because the more intuitive, non-dominant hemisphere of the child's brain has a greater 'say' in matters until the so-called dominant and decidedly more rational hemisphere takes over. This change takes place when language and reading skills are developing, generally from the age of five years and on (Joseph 1992, pp.87, 95; Joseph 2004).

The ability to perceive information outside of the normal channels is a facet of what we call intuition. As with any skill, the more familiar we are with it, the more we trust and appreciate it. Sadly, the converse is also true. Many adults, particularly men, do not or are unable to 'tune into' their intuition, and for them it is, as Albert Einstein said, a forgotten gift. Young children and those confronting death are the notable exceptions. Children are naturally intuitive and are comfortable with their feelings; so much so they have little hesitation in saying how they feel. The dying resemble children in their ability to intuit messages and express feelings and commonly resort to symbolism and metaphor as a means of describing what is otherwise ineffable. It is often the only way they can effectively communicate their lived experience: 'I'm at the end of the road' or 'I feel as if I have been hit by a bus'.

Unless family, friends and health care workers are attuned to this type of language, the messages will fall on deaf ears.

The following remarkable stories were shared during 'Conscious Living, Conscious Dying' workshops conducted by Ann and myself. Based on the emotional response of the person telling the story, there was little reason to doubt their veracity.

A three-year-old said to her pregnant mother, 'Our baby has gone to be with Mandy' (Mandy was the mother's sister, who had died some months earlier). 'No' said the mother, 'the baby is fine.' The mother had a routine ultrasound the following day and the baby was found to be dead.

A five-year-old boy said to his mother, 'Don't be upset if I die.' His mother was shocked by what she heard and said, 'You won't die; you are only five.' He was killed in a motor vehicle accident several weeks later.

A young boy started talking to his parents about his fear of death and what might happen to him after death. They were alarmed and unsure how to respond. Several weeks later he told his parents he was no longer afraid of death. He died unexpectedly later that same day.

We could rationalise each of these stories and put them down to coincidence simply because that is the most comfortable way of dealing with situations or events that make no sense. What we need to confront is the possibility of acquiring information or knowledge that is independent of the senses. All of us regularly intuit or perceive things, but as the message is subtle, we are not always aware of it, just as we are unaware of much of the information that floods our ordinary senses. Not a day goes by without each of us intuiting messages about ourselves or others; messages that are frequently overlooked because our rational mind is overloaded or preoccupied. This highway of perception is often referred to as the 'sixth' sense. Ann and I learnt a powerful and unforgettable lesson from not following our intuition.

> *Many years ago, our eldest daughter, Claire, then aged six, was referred to an eye specialist. After several cancelled appointments Ann and I decided there could be no further excuses. An appointment was made for later that week and our neighbour agreed to baby sit our four-week-old daughter, Moira. On the morning of the appointment Ann felt uneasy about going and wondered if she should cancel the appointment once again. As there was no logical reason to explain her dis-ease she took Moira to the neighbour's house and then headed off with Claire to the appointment. The uneasy feeling steadily built and by the time the visit had concluded it was overpowering. Ann drove home much faster than usual and as she turned into the road that led home she saw our neighbour running towards her with Moira cradled in her arms. Ann did not have to be told; she knew immediately that Moira had died. Only then did she understand the subtle message she had intuited all that morning.*

As our experience indicates, the message that intuition brings is far from clear. We sense something but do not understand what it is 'saying'. The message we intuit is not a delusion. It is, according to the great sage Yogananda, the face-to-face knowledge of reality without any intermediary (1995, p.118). It is a message we perceive with our whole being rather than through any particular sense organ and because it bypasses our conscious rational mind, the message often escapes our attention.

Intuition is heightened when we are confronted by illness or impending death. Unfortunately, it is often drowned out and cannot be heard when the mind is overwhelmed by emotions or when attempting to deal with hard facts that are continually presented to it. The following analogy from Grahame Jones' book *Magnanimous Despair* not only tells us about his experiences with his own life-threatening illness, but also illustrates how symbolism can plumb the depth of our emotions and intuition. In Grahame's case it also predicted, with great accuracy what was to unfold. He says, 'I recall the little Dutch boy at the dyke cleverly holding back the mighty flood with his finger. I, too, feel like the little Dutch boy. With my hands I am reaching out to cover the cracks in the wall. But as I hold out at full stretch, I do so with fear, the knowledge that another break will come, somewhere beyond my reach and at a moment when both hands are already engaged elsewhere' (1998, p.9).

Intuition is our best guide at times of stress and when we are dying. It will only be heard, however, if we eliminate the static that arises from the fearful mind and tune into that 'still quiet voice within'. Intuition constantly communicates with those who are dying but the peace and quiet required for it to be heard is often hard to come by, particularly in hospitals.

Solutions to problems, flashes of genius, profound realisations or 'gut' feelings frequently surface during times of daydreaming or first thing in the morning when the rational mind is not fully awake. In my case it is often during my early morning jogs. Indeed many of the concepts espoused in this book arose from the deep recesses of my mind while jogging or while musing. What continues to surprise me, however, is not that this happens but how my opinion of the *in-sights* change once the rational mind comes into play.

The dying are very much like children in that they are surprisingly astute and intuit subtle messages better than most others. They can see beneath the surface and are often more aware of what another feels but are reluctant to share. Depending on who it is, this lack of congruence may trouble the dying person and further compounds their suffering. I have seen family conflicts unsuccessfully hidden from a dying relative who could sense the tension without being told of it. Some who are dying will cling to life because they feel their family is not yet ready to let go. Others welcome death not only as a release from their suffering but also because they sense their ongoing suffering compounds that of those they love. A dying woman whose family had unsuccessfully tried to hide their grief from her once said to me, 'It's not the cancer that's killing me but the way it's tearing my family apart.'

Although much has been written about the subject, we have little knowledge about how, where and why intuition arises. Sacred texts and Eastern philosophy are perhaps the best sources of knowledge but they deal with the subject in an esoteric or experiential way that is often hard to understand. The great spiritual teacher Yogananda lists five levels of intuition (1995, pp.236-239). They are:

- knowledge that I exist
- the immediate knowledge of vital life forces
- direct knowledge of the mind
- direct knowledge of the intellect
- direct knowledge of bliss.

In everyday life, intuition is drowned out by the senses and the intellect (this is often referred to as body consciousness) and only approaches its zenith when free of these restraints, as is the case with disembodied consciousness (Yogananda 1995, p.411). Bliss is not easily attained in our modern world but can occur spontaneously in a diluted form with Maslow's 'peak experiences' or with intense spiritual practices such as meditation, contemplation or prayer. The earlier planes of intuition that Yogananda described are more accessible than the more profound levels, but the rewards are proportionally less.

Many end-of-life experiences described in this book are examples of disembodied consciousness. The ineffability that accompanies these not only reflects a blissful state but also the enormous potential for healing that is available when someone is dying. The potential to experience disembodied consciousness is greatest when a person can transcend emotions and thoughts. In the context of dying, this state is not easily attained, but is more likely if adequate preparation for death has been made and the person is cared for in a supportive, compassionate and peaceful environment. If we accept this, caring for the dying takes on a whole new dimension, with the goal of spiritual comfort as important as pain relief. On this matter Paul Beirne says, 'In one's final days, peace and harmony are life-sustaining values. They offer essential sustenance to the spirit as the body weakens' (Beirne 2002, p.140).

Similarities between the planes of intuition described by Yogananda and the many experiences of dying suggest there is a connection between the two and that, progress through this hierarchy is possible when care is holistic. I will list the five levels of intuition described by Yogananda (in italics) and follow each with a brief description of how this form of intuition might manifest in those who are dying.

Knowledge that I exist. Knowledge of existence is very real for those who are dying for they know their life is drawing to an end. The healthy rarely give much thought to what existence means, but for those who are confronted by the reality of death, life is precious and existence is not taken for granted. This sentiment was expressed particularly well by Treya Wilber who, just months before her death from breast cancer, said, 'Because I can no longer ignore death I pay more attention to life' (Wilber and Wilber 2001, p.360). The experience of life or living another day, brings a certain joy to those who are dying, but it also brings its share of sadness. Every moment of every day becomes precious.

The immediate knowledge of 'pranic' energy or vital life forces. This force is well recognised in many of the Eastern traditions and referred to as chi or prana. Western culture has no specific name for it other than 'life force' and only acknowledges it in daily life with comments such as 'I am full of beans' or 'I am drained of energy'. We notice the extremes of energy and anything in between often passes below the radar. This is true for most but not all people. Those who engage in meditation, yoga, prayer or other spiritual practices learn to tune into this subtle force and the most adept sometimes detect imbalances or blocks in the energy flow which, they believe, cause or predispose to illness. Acupuncture, yoga, Reiki and similar practices are used to address these imbalances and are also used prophylactically to maintain good health.

Whether we are aware of it or not, this vital force is present throughout life and keeps every cell within our body pulsing with energy. In Western societies, this vital force is commonly appreciated only when it is in short supply, as with physical, emotional, mental or spiritual crises. If the illness is acute, the loss of energy is temporary and vitality quickly returns. The situation with a life-limiting illness is clearly different. As health deteriorates, vitality wanes and this manifests as progressive weakness, inanition and, ultimately, death. The dying are acutely aware of their life force ebbing away and can sometimes predict the time of their death more accurately than the attending doctor. Paradoxically, some of the senses (touch and hearing) become hyper-acute as the life force is slowly extinguished. This is why family and carers are urged to maintain some form of physical and vocal contact with a dying person even though they may appear to be 'unconscious'.

Bob was an elderly man dying from cancer. He was unconscious and death was expected in a matter of hours. The family had gathered around his bedside and, being of a Catholic tradition, they chanted the rosary. When they finished Bill was heard to say, 'Amen'.

At this level of intuition, it is not only the physical senses that are heightened but also a person's awareness of what is happening to them and around them. They are aware of other people's thoughts and emotions, even if these people are outside their immediate presence. This may explain why someone who is unconscious can cling to life until a much loved friend or relative arrives. It may also be the reason why the dying choose the time of their death. Sometimes this is when the immediate family is present, but it can also be when the family leaves the room, often for the first time in days. The latter situation usually results in family distress when it may be the dying person's final gift.

Direct knowledge of mind, its effects and its combinations with other principles of perception and cognition. At this level of intuition the dying person is more in tune with their and other people's physical and emotional state. If free of pain and cared for in a healing space the dying person often accepts the inevitability of death and approaches it with a greater sense of peace. They benefit from having those around them who accept rather than deny or resist what is meant to be. The truth of this is reflected in the dying words of Robert Kavanaugh. He said, 'I found that those around me who were not busy running from their fears could be my closest and only effective friends as death came near' (1974, p.57).

Direct knowledge of the intellect manifesting as wisdom and an ability to discern truth. This is a time when a dying person is more often asleep than awake. Apart from being in tune with their inner world and innate wisdom they are also free of the troubled mind and dying body that otherwise dominates their life. Because of this, the likelihood of near-to-death experiences increases substantially.

Metaphorically speaking, it is as if they have removed a tight shoe and can now expand into superconsciousness.

Direct knowledge of bliss. To experience bliss at the time of death may seem as unlikely as it is incredible. The bliss Yogananda refers to is not simply happiness but a state of peace that springs from a combination of acceptance and forgiveness and manifests as unconditional love. Such love knows no bounds. This experience of love does not depend on religious beliefs or a belief in an afterlife. It is not contingent on making one's peace with others or with God, but comes from making peace with themselves.

After-death communication

Mystical experiences come not from a sudden possession of a higher power but by a suspension of the normal everyday habit of perceiving or knowing

GUY CLAXTON
Noises from the Darkroom 1994

In 1971 Doctor Dewi Rees, a little known general practitioner, created quite a stir when he published a report detailing the result of interviews with widows and widowers who lived in a small but well-defined area of Wales. Of the 293 people he interviewed, almost half had experienced what he described as 'hallucinations of widowhood' (now called after-death communication). The most common experience reported was a strong sense (and a belief) that the deceased spouse was close at hand. Visions, hearing their voice or the feeling of being touched were also described. In many cases the hallucinations occurred, not once but intermittently over many years. Even though most said the experience assisted them in their grief, few had previously spoken of it, fearing something so intensely personal and significant would be trivialised. Rees concluded, 'Hallucinations are normal experiences after widowhood, providing helpful psychological support to those experiencing them' (Rees 1971, p.41).

Rees was not the first to observe this phenomenon but it was he who brought after-death communication into the public arena, normalised the experience and liberated many who were grieving from the thought that they were going mad. While many of his findings have not been replicated (Datson and Marwit 1997), the scientific community now accepts that the experiences described by Rees do occur and are not pathological but are part of the normal grieving process occurring in psychologically healthy, high-functioning individuals (Ross and Joshi 1992). What precipitates the experience, however, is far from resolved.

Two hundred years earlier a Swiss philosopher by the name of Charles Bonnet described complex visual hallucinations in blind or partially blind adults who were grieving the loss of a loved one. The visions were commonly of the person who had died. This phenomenon, called the Charles Bonnet Syndrome occurs in approximately 12 per cent of the blind population with most of the hallucinations occurring during periods of low-level arousal (Teunisse et al. 1996). Many of Bonnet's original observations have since been questioned. A review by Teunisse confirmed that visual hallucinations were not uncommon amongst the blind or partially blind, but only 2 per cent were of a deceased family member.

In the majority of instances the hallucination was of a person or scene that was mundane and ordinary. Many were irritated by the frequency of the visions and hoped they would go away. A small number were so distressed they turned to medication as a means of suppressing them. All this contrasts sharply with what we know about after-death communication and, despite the earlier observations made by Bonnet, the evidence now weighs heavily against any connection between a Charles Bonnet-like syndrome and after-death communication.

The more plausible theory is a variant of that used to explain deathbed visions (Chapter 1). As with the latter, intense life-like dreams while asleep or while daydreaming can wake the bereaved from their slumber, and because they are so vivid and life-like they are experienced as real rather than imagined. Rees found that the majority of hallucinations took place during the day with only 17 percent occurring at night or at transitional sleep/wake times. When the experience occurred during the day, solitude, a relaxed body and quiet mind created the ideal conditions for the experience to occur. In real life this can be while the bereaved person is sitting quietly, musing, meditating, praying, lying in bed or engaged in mundane activities such as preparing a meal or washing dishes.

It took almost four years in palliative care before I was graced with a grieving relative's experience of an after-death communication. As much as time will allow, I now pay a courtesy visit to all grieving families and during that visit I ask if anyone has had an unusual experience involving their deceased relative. The bereaved are more than willing and are greatly relieved to share any treasured moment if they believe the enquiry is genuine. Otherwise they will keep it to themselves, fearing they might be labelled insane.

Here are a few examples of what grieving family have shared with me:

- He told us to move on with our lives. He said he was okay and loved us very much.
- My father appeared while I slept and said goodbye.
- Nick woke and as he walked down the hall he saw Rusty standing in front of him. He was stunned and remained frozen to the spot. He was unsure how long the vision lasted but thinks it was brief. Nothing was said but Nick was absolutely clear about the message Rusty delivered: 'You are the only man in this family. Please take care of my wife and daughters.'

The communication may occur just once or several times and usually, but not always, within the first three months of their loved one's death. It is mostly a subtle impression of the person being close by, but sometimes the connection is more life-like, with the grieving person seeing their departed loved one, hearing their voice or feeling as though they are being touched or stroked by them. Less commonly there may be unexplained events such as a clock's stopping, unusual noises or mysterious breakages (Fenwick & Fenwick 2008). At first, the person may be unsettled by what is happening, but with time or subsequent communications the anxiety that may have been present is replaced by a sense of peace and gratitude.

What about those who do not have any form of after-death contact? Their grief is often be exacerbated when they hear of others who have had the type of contact that they long to experience. In their vulnerable state they may feel forgotten or abandoned. Allowing them to talk about this can be helpful and may be all that is required. It is the talking rather than the search for answers that is most helpful.

It is a compliment if someone speaks to you about an after-death communication. Your only task is to listen and allow the person to tell their story free of interruptions. Their incident needs to be heard, validated and normalised by indicating that such experiences are common and are a normal part of the grieving process. If there is some aspect of the experience that troubles them, let them talk about it. You are not expected to provide answers, for indeed there may be no answers. Just simply be there and allow the other person to share the experience.

Chapter 5

As the sun sets

Death is the side of life
which is turned away from us
and upon which we shed no light.

RAINER MARIA RILKE

Chapter 5

As the sun sets

Early in my medical career I had the privilege of hearing a 90-year-old doctor talk about his years in medical practice that stretched as far back as WW1. In those days there were no antibiotics to treat infection, no insulin for diabetes, or medications for common ailments such as angina, hypertension, cardiac failure and asthma. There was no dialysis for renal failure, no oxygen for respiratory disease and no treatment for heart attacks other than morphine. More often than not he presided over the death of young and old with nothing more to offer than pain relief and his comforting presence.

Medicine has come a long way since then and we in the 21st century are indeed fortunate to be the beneficiaries of its many advances. Illnesses that were once fatal are now curable and life for those who have an incurable illness can be prolonged by any number of measures that include, chemotherapeutic agents, radiotherapy, transplant surgery, renal dialysis, cardiac pacemakers, cardiac surgery and endless other innovative treatments. The following quote from Daniel Callahan, however, suggests that progress, has come at a cost: 'The enhanced biological knowledge and technological skill has served to make our dying all the more problematic: harder to predict, more difficult to manage, the source of more moral dilemmas and nasty choices, and spiritually more productive of anguish, ambivalence, and uncertainty' (Callahan 1993, p.33). Many more lives are saved, but medicine as practiced today struggles to adequately and appropriately care for the dying. As the capacity to treat disease improved, medicine's focus was less on dying and more on its prevention (Ashby 2009). This is not a criticism, but a simple acknowledgement that medicine's raison d'être now is to keep people alive, something doctors do with enormous skill and unquestionable dedication.

Death is a relative stranger to many of us and our knowledge of it comes principally through the media rather than first-hand experience. It is, as Rilke says, 'The side of life which is turned away from us.' Few in today's society have sat with someone as they were dying. When they do, death 'comes to life' and they get to know it for the first time. They feel its presence – the totality of the emotions that accompany it – and are overwhelmed by it. A sense of impotence and helplessness arises which drives many to do anything that might stop death in its tracks. Diets, vitamins, alternative treatments, herbal medicines and prayer are frequently summoned. At the same time the medical profession delves deeper into its treatment armoury in the hope of finding something that may prevent or delay the inevitable. Death has become the enemy.

While the nightly news regularly exposes death, often with graphic footage, it remains at arm's length and we rarely feel emotion unless the death is particularly traumatic or involves someone we know. In other stories, new and promising treatments are unveiled and lull us into believing that a cure for most illnesses is only a matter of time. This creates a myth that death happens only to others and if perchance we or someone we know becomes ill then a cure must certainly exist or is close at hand. The healthy and the not-so-healthy develop a false sense of security and ultimately a denial of death itself. Referring once again to Rilke, 'We shed no light [on death].'

Dying in the 21st century is very different from how it was for that ninety-year old doctor. It has become anything but straightforward or predictable. Now, it is not uncommon to see those at the edge of death connected to a variety of tubes while drugs continue to be administered and monitors tell us all is not yet lost (Fins 1999; Middlewood 2001). These well-intentioned interventions rarely alter the course of events and in most situations succeed only in prolonging the dying and giving false hope to those who sit by the bedside. This is not meant as criticism, but only to show how dying in the 21st century is, as Callahan stated, harder to predict and the source of endless choices and dilemmas for all involved.

It comes as no surprise then to realise that care of those with a life-threatening illness has taken on the guise of a battle, with death as the unseen enemy. If medicine wins, the pain and setbacks along the way and the toll on the patient and family are worthwhile.

Failure, however, tells another story. When death is the victor, there has to be a vanquished and that, I believe, is not how any of us would wish our death to be seen. I suspect all would prefer to leave this world with a sense of having completed their lives rather than feeling defeated by death.

If death is seen as the enemy, it will always be met with resistance. If we accept it as the natural end to life then we are more likely to respect it and be better prepared for when the bell tolls. Not so many years ago a high infant mortality rate meant that many children died early in life. Most of these deaths occurred at home with parents and doctors helpless to do anything but sit, wait and watch. As painful as this was, families knew what to expect. Rather than engage in a battle, they prepared for the death of their child as best they could and journeyed with them to the very end. Nothing obscured their view of death.

I am not suggesting we yield to death whenever it threatens. Medicine has come a long way and it is incumbent on the medical profession to do all it can to prevent death. Society rightly expects nothing less. There comes a time, however, when efforts to prolong life are futile and counterproductive. This is when the battle must end and when preparation for death and saying good-bye become more important. Because this feels like giving up, many recoil from the thought of it and prefer that the medical profession continue its fight until the bitter end.

The major difficulty here is not the decision to change direction but to know when this time has arrived and how best to navigate the emotionally-charged terrain that accompanies the decision. There is no simple formula but honest and on-going communication involving the medical team, the patient and family is where it all starts. In some circumstances the presence of an independent person acting as an advocate and support can be helpful. This could be the family doctor, a minister, priest, pastoral care worker or social worker and their task is to ensure the family hear and understand what is being said and to offer emotional support. They fulfill a role of old – the Amicus Mortis or Death Doula – the friend of the dying.

Why, you may be wondering, should we call an end to the battle? Isn't it better to fight to the bitter end and follow Dylan Thomas's invocation, 'Do not go gentle into that good night; rage, rage against the dying of the light.' There is no right or wrong way to die. We will each die our own death in our own unique way. All I wish to point out is that there is no defeat or failure in saying, 'It's time to stop'. To do so is an extraordinary declaration of love, strength and courage, for it allows family and carers to focus on what is real. It helps all those involved to move from a forlorn hope of prolonging life to the reality of impending death. It removes uncertainty but not anguish, for nothing can extinguish the pain of loss. It is a necessary journey we must all one day undertake. It is the wisdom of dying.

How you can best assist

There is much that can be done to ensure this emotionally charged journey is imbued with tenderness, love and respect and is remembered not as failure but as closure. Control of pain and other distressing symptoms is important, but this responsibility falls to others. The role of family is to ensure, as much as possible, that the dying person's wishes are respected and that there is ample opportunity to give and receive love. Listen carefully to what they say and search carefully for symbolic meanings when words make no apparent sense. Do not be afraid to consult the oracle of their dreams and pay careful attention to the wisdom that springs from your intuition. Be prepared for the possibility of a deathbed vision and respond openly and gently to this and all other challenges that arise as your loved one's life draws to an end.

If you bring this level of awareness to the dying process you may soften some of the fear and anxiety that you and your loved one will inevitably experience. You may also rid yourself of the helplessness that frequently accompanies the care of someone who is dying. In this way, your loved one's death will not be regarded as a failure but as an epic journey made possible by the love and care you showered upon them. Death is not some point on the horizon upon which we focus all our attention. Dying is a minute by minute experience, replete with highs and lows that demands our love and full attention if we are to navigate the course it has set.

Being with someone as they die is one of the hardest and most painful things you will be asked to do, yet it is a most wonderful gift that you can offer. It involves sitting with your loved one and the ever-lengthening shadow death casts over you and those close to you. The task is not easy, even for those who have been there many times before.

Several years ago I completed a unit of Clinical Pastoral Education in a large Sydney hospital. The task involved sitting with people who had a life-threatening illness and the only expectation was to be a companion to them. Having been a palliative care doctor for many years I had seen a lot of death and thought the task would be relatively easy. How wrong I was. It was one of the hardest things I have ever done. I was not at all comfortable with my helplessness and my inability to do something. In my pastoral role I had none of the usual doctor tools, resources or jargon to fall back on. There were no prescriptions I could write or assurances to give. I was stripped of all the crutches I normally relied upon to support me during these difficult encounters. Death will expose your helplessness and vulnerability, just as it did mine, but in so doing it often reveals previously unknown strength. It may seem paradoxical but, your power lies in your willingness to be vulnerable.

Creating a healing space

When talking about death, the idea of a healing space may seem absurd. The confusion arises because most consider healing and curing to be the same thing, when they are almost polar opposites. Healing comes from within whereas curing comes from without; people heal themselves while the act of curing is something done by another (usually a doctor). Healing involves a positive and often dramatic shift in one's emotional and spiritual well-being whereas curing results in an improvement in a person's physical status. Doctors may cure an illness but only a 'patient' can heal themselves. It may seem unbelievable, but healing is possible when cure is impossible provided there is sufficient time and opportunity for this miracle to unfold.

While healing can sometimes occur of its own accord, it is more likely to arise if the space surrounding the person is conducive to healing. We call this space a healing environment and contrary to expectations the most important space you can prepare is not what you create around you but within you (Miller 2001). The frame of mind you are in when you enter any room has a far greater healing potential than anything you can do to improve the physical ambience. So, time spent in preparing is time well spent. Seek to cultivate love, empty yourself of any emotional baggage, forget the woes of the day and enter into that space free of all agendas other than that of being totally present, aware and real.

The quality of your presence is not measured by the length of your visit but by the measure of your authenticity. It is not easy work, but it is rewarding, so take time after any visit to reflect. Do not be too harsh on yourself if you have said things you wish you hadn't. Always remember that a dying person is attuned to and responds to your authenticity more than the words you use. Their intuitive knowing allows them to see beneath the surface. You may say something you wish you hadn't, but if the dying person feels your love, the words are unimportant.

When you enter the room of someone who is at the edge of death you are entering a sacred space. It is a space where authenticity, love and compassion reign supreme, but never at the expense of laughter, joy and the occasional irreverence. It is sacred simply because it is a place of healing.

There are of course many things that can be done to the physical space that contribute to this sacredness, provided of course it is consistent with the expressed or known wishes of the dying person. This may include music, photos, pictures, children's or grandchildren's drawings. To be surrounded by things that are familiar and significant is not only comforting to the person who is dying, it also reminds them and others of their uniqueness.

Noise can compromise this healing space. A dying person's hearing is hyper-acute and is, we are told, one of the last senses to go. Noise that is sudden, loud or jarring can jolt them out of their peaceful state, a space that is often laced with dreams or deathbed visions. So make every attempt to ensure the environment is peaceful. That does not necessarily mean noise-free, but only that the sounds are comforting and familiar.

When death is imminent, the environment may need to change. What may have been appropriate earlier on may be inappropriate when a person is unresponsive. This is the time for ritual. Prayer, song, music, readings, loving words or tender touches have their place, but so too does silence. All of this honours the dying person and also respects the significance, richness and mystery of this time. It is the time when the dying person prepares to leave their body and when deathbed visions commonly occur. It is the labour phase of dying and, as with birth, there is that strange but beautiful admixture of extraordinary pain and exquisite love.

Creating a healing space is not only beneficial for the dying person but also for others who share the space. Not so long ago I was the doctor caring for Sue, a young mother dying of cancer. She had been unwell and confined to her bed for many months. In this time her husband and two young children had gone to great efforts to make her room the centre of the home. The children gathered by her bed before and after school and spent much of their spare time in the bed with her. They often ate in that room, watched television and did their homework under her watchful eye. The bed faced a northern window affording her a sunny outlook and an uninterrupted view of the trees outside. The room was bright and overflowing with love, laughter, joy and sadness. It was a living space, a place where emotions bubbled away and often surfaced in the form of tears and laughter. It was a healing space for all.

Sue's condition suddenly deteriorated and in a matter of days she became unconscious. The change in her physical condition devastated her husband and children for what had, for many years been expected, was now real. No longer able to communicate with their mother, the children looked on helplessly as a previously agreed transfer to the palliative care unit was enacted. I wondered what could be done to make this time meaningful rather than the cold, clinical and painful separation that it seemed to be. I rang my wife Ann and sought her advice. She was a palliative care volunteer and knew Sue and her family well.

Ann arrived, and with the family gathered as many flowers and candles as they could muster. These were spread around the room and the candles lit. The children chose their favourite poem and read it to their mother before giving her a good-bye kiss. This very simple ceremony had a profound effect on the children and their father. Enormous sadness pervaded the room but the sense of helplessness had been overcome. The children visited their mother every day in the palliative care unit until she died. They always arrived with a book under their arm and would read to her for much of their visit. The little home ceremony had obviously rubbed off on them and I would like to think that the daily reading ritual was as healing for Sue as it was for her children, her husband and their extended family.

Unconsciousness

Although Sue was unconscious for the last few days of her life I have little doubt that she was aware of her children's visits and their readings. The word *unconscious* suggests that Sue and others like her have no awareness of their outer or inner world. In other words they are shut off from the world of sensations and emotions. We now know this to be false, with up to 80 per cent of people who recover from an episode of unconsciousness saying they have some memory of that period (Lawrence 1995, 1997). William James tells us that unconsciousness is not the absence of consciousness but, 'a potential form of consciousness entirely different' (1985, p.388). On a related note, the philosopher and teacher, Michael Grosso says that a weakening of ordinary waking consciousness is almost a prerequisite for archetypal experiences including dreams and near-to-death experiences (Bailey and Yates 1996, p.133).

There is now strong evidence to support the belief that unconsciousness which precedes death is more akin to sleep. In this sleep-like state people can dream, open their eyes, hear and experience pain. Their level of awareness varies from a very deep sleep to times of being almost fully alert. The wide-awake state is infrequent, lasts a variable period of time and is always a great surprise to those by the bedside (MacLeod 2009). Explanations for this waking up before death include unrelieved pain and the experience of a deathbed vision. We also know that unconscious patients can wake when a much loved relative arrives or because of something that is said. Having been unconscious for several days, one of my patients woke after being told it was her birthday. She sat up, sipped champagne and after several hours lapsed back into unconsciousness and died shortly afterwards.

The use of the word unconscious is misleading and is used in the medical setting simply to describe a person who is unresponsive. It does not mean they cannot hear, do not feel pain, or that they will never open their eyes, move a limb, utter a word or shed a tear. If anything they are *superconscious* and are capable of sensing more than we can possibly know and of engaging the real world with a word, by opening their eyes or squeezing another's hand. At other times they escape into the mystery of a dream or a deathbed vision, both of which contribute, in their own way to healing, even at this late stage of life.

> *Lorna had been unconscious for several days and her family, believing that she was suffering, wondered if anything could be done to ease her pain and to speed up the dying process. The nurse calmly responded to this veiled request for euthanasia by saying their mother was 'hanging on' until she received a phone call from her son who, for personal reasons, was unable to be at the bedside. Knowing their mother had not responded to their presence for several days most of the family found this hard to believe, but accepted it nonetheless. Four hours later the phone rang. After confirming it was her brother,*

Lorna's daughter put the phone to her mother's ear. No one could hear what the son said but tears welled up in Lorna's eyes and as soon as the call finished, Lorna took her last breath.

Several years ago the Queensland *Sunday Mail* ran an article titled 'A matter of life and death' in which they reported one man's experience of being in a coma for a period of one month (The Sunday Mail October 8, 2006, p. 52). The following excerpts are experiences described by the man while he was in this seemingly unconscious state:

It was a bewildering, alien sensation of things being done to me by forces I could not see...if the nurses had not warned my apparently deaf ears of what they were going to do, I think I would have been scared indeed.

I did not merely passively receive information. Inside my comatose [unconscious] body I was consciously planning how to break out.

The people who visited me wove themselves into the dream, and I knew who had sent me messages and roughly what they had said.

What made the big difference was my dear wife's presence. I could feel her hand in mine, our fingers entwined. I knew it was her, though I could not figure out what she was doing in these strange worlds.

> *At one stage…I even felt as if I was in the antechamber of some great room. The door never opened and I never saw behind it, but I had a strong sense that was where the real action was.*
>
> *She [the patient's wife] recounted how our son's godmother, though a vegetarian, had gone so far as to cook a chicken…When I awoke, I amazed everybody by repeating this story in detail.*

In my work I am constantly reminded of the mystery of the so-called unconscious state. Opening of the eyes is so common that I always alert family to the possibility, knowing it could surprise or trouble them if they are not forewarned. I frequently hear stories of unconscious people close to death saying 'Amen' at the conclusion of a prayer session or inserting a one word response to a bedside conversation even though they had been unresponsive for days. Perhaps the most mysterious event of all is the waking, similar to Hazel's (Chapter 1) that can occur at the point of death. That this should happen when the body is at death's door is nothing short of a mystery and raises questions concerning the widely held belief that consciousness is a by-product of the brain's function (Nadeau and Kafatos 1999; Lorimer 1990).

There is an abundance of literature to support the belief that people who are unconscious, even those receiving medication, can hear, yet very few in the wider community are aware of this. Medical, nursing and hospital staff, family and friends need to be reminded of this to ensure all conversations are inclusive of and appropriate for the dying person. In palliative care, the rule is, always speak to the unconscious person and not about them. So if you enter the room of someone who is unconscious, introduce yourself, orientate them to the time and the day, talk to them about your visit and what you plan to do while you are there. Whatever you say, make it brief and use touch as a means of re-enforcing the connection. The unconscious person values your presence, but at this time in their life they will appreciate your loving company more than a lengthy conversation.

All that has been said about the care of someone who is unconscious applies equally to those with a history of dementia. What they experience when they are dying is determined by the degree of cognitive impairment immediately prior to their terminal phase. They certainly experience pain, but their understanding of what has been said will parallel that which existed beforehand. The same applies to their ability to recognise and respond to music, touch and other forms of sensory stimulation as well as the likelihood of them having a deathbed vision.

It is well-accepted that the amount of time spent in REM sleep diminishes with increasing dementia. If the dream theory of deathbed visions is correct then the likelihood of a deathbed vision occurring during, as well as before the phase of unconsciousness diminishes as their dementia worsens. With some forms of dementia, however, the acting out of dreams (referred to as REM sleep behaviour disorder) is not uncommon and can sometimes be responsible for movements and behavioural changes during the period of unconsciousness. This is particularly true for those who exhibited such sleep disturbances earlier in their illness. The important point being that restlessness in dementia patients who are unconscious can be due to any number of factors including unrelieved pain, REM sleep behaviour disorder or a deathbed vision.

Unconsciousness is the final step in a dying person's preparation for death. There are many factors that influence the duration of unconsciousness, but in the palliative care situation it may, depending on circumstances, be as short as one hour or as long as a week. Some defy the odds and live for much longer than anyone had imagined possible, while others slip away suddenly and almost without any warning. The time of death is unpredictable and apart from changes in skin colour and the pattern of breathing there are no reliable clues as to when it may occur. What needs to be emphasised is that medication administered at this time, provided it is given in appropriate doses and for the right reasons, does not shorten life. It only ensures the person remains pain free and comfortable.

Often, a person dies when no one is present. In some instances this happens when family members leave the room briefly, having spent hours or days in vigil beforehand. The family often wonder if this is pure coincidence or whether the unconscious person has chosen to do it this way, and if so, why? Dying when no one is present may be that person's final gift to the family they love and while many find this hard to accept it is a possibility that cannot be excluded. The explanation may be found within the adage, 'most people die the way they have lived'. If this is the case then those who have an independent nature, a tendency to do things alone or who always think of others may, at some deep instinctive level, choose to die alone. The opportunity for family to reflect on such a possibility can sometimes bring a degree of acceptance and peace to a situation that might otherwise become an added source of grief.

At a more esoteric level, it is possible that a loving presence can still be felt despite that person being physically absent. This is more likely to be true when the familial and emotional bond is strong or when time and effort have been dedicated to creating a healing space. The dying person may be *superconscious* and highly attuned to this form of communication and to those who create it. This may seem improbable, but a study using brain imaging has shown changes within the brain of subjects when another person sent peaceful thoughts to them from some distant location. The areas of the subject's brain that were activated involved functions that included self-reflection, decision making and comfort (Achterberg 2005).

Dying can also be protracted even with those who appear to be at death's door. This is disconcerting for a family who have been told or who expected their loved to have died beforehand. They are often left wondering if their relative is as close to death as others have suggested. They may even entertain the thought that he/she is waiting for someone to arrive or that they need a comforting or reassuring message before they can let go. We cannot know what is going on in the mind of someone close to death. A slow death is not always a sign the person is waiting for something or someone or that they need permission to move on. Telling the unconscious person it is okay to die has, however, become a fashion. This may be appropriate when it is done by immediate family, preferably the next of kin, and that the words are carefully selected and the message is not repeated too often. It is less appropriate for non-family members to do so, but there may be circumstances when others may take on this role. This may be when the dying person has no living relatives.

Because deathbed visions are common at this time, words that acknowledge this possibility may also be appropriate. These may include messages such as, 'follow the light' or 'if you see (name of a pre-deceased loved one) take their hand and let them show you the way'. Metaphors can also be powerful particularly if they symbolise an aspect of the person's life that they can readily relate to. For a bushwalker one can say, 'follow the track', for a surfer, 'it's time to catch your last wave' and for someone who has laboured hard, 'you can now rest'. What you say should always be made optional and you can indicate this with words like, 'when you are ready' or 'maybe it is time to...'

If having done all these things the person continues to hang onto life, the possibility of their waiting for somebody or something should then be entertained and acted upon even if it is only remotely possible. If there is no obvious reason, be patient and accepting, support one another, take time out and remember everyone dies their own death and they will do it their own way.

Tim lay dying in his bed at home. I and the family were surprised he had survived this long. He had been unconscious with nothing to drink for several days. When the family asked 'Why is this taking so long?' I had no answer other than to suggest that Tim had his reasons and that one day they might understand. He died several days later. It was 3 pm on a Friday. As we sat contemplating the occasion, his eldest daughter jumped up and announced, 'I know why Dad took so long to die.' Everyone waited with bated breath. She continued, 'At work, Dad always left his difficult decisions to 3 pm on Fridays.' This was accepted with great laughter and relief.

The moment of death

Death is the full-stop to the life sentence

PHILLIP ADAMS

As a person approaches the moment of death their body's metabolism gradually winds down until it ceases altogether. At that exact moment the heart beat and respirations cease, the pulse disappears and the circulation comes to a sudden halt. The body is deprived of its vital fuel – oxygen – and the systems and organs that naturally depend on it cease to function. This is death in its rawest and most clinical form, and would appear to justify the graphic description given by Phillip Adams. But, what of the brain?

Until recent times, the assumption has been that the brain follows the same path as other organs and that it too grinds to a halt. At the moment of death, all electrical activity within the brain ceases and the electroencephalogram which records brain activity is said to 'flat line'. The so-called waking or lightening up (Chapter 3) and deathbed visions immediately before death (Chapter1) are not quite in keeping with this hypothesis, but it was not until recent times when research demonstrated a sudden surge of electrical activity at or immediately after clinical death did the 'grinding down' theory start to unravel (Barbato 2001; Chawla 2009; Auyong 2010)).

The cause of this surge was initially attributed to the last agonal throws of a dying brain secondary to chaotic and disorganized brain activity at that time. Recent studies involving animals and humans, and utilizing sophisticated brain monitoring equipment (electroencephalogram) demonstrate that the surge is caused by a coordinated brain wave (high frequency gamma oscillations) that appears at the time of or immediately after the person has died. The most interesting thing about these gamma oscillations is that they are usually associated with an alert and fully awake state (Chawla 2009; Borjigin 2013) such as being in the zone (Stokes & Voytek). Similar patterns have also been found in experienced meditators as they meditated on love and compassion.

While it is still early days, the research suggests this surge of electrical activity at or immediately after the moment of death may not only explain events such as waking/lightening up, deathbed visions and near-death experiences but it also gives us reason to hope that peace at the moment of death may be a reality and not just wishful thinking.

Chapter 6

After the sun has set

The material empirical human being is an outer covering that with its suffocating deceptive coils envelops the chrysalis of a new reality: the inner person, the true essential person.

JACQUES LACARRIENE
The Gnostics

Chapter 6

After the sun has set

I recently attended the funeral of one of my patients. Fred was only 47 when he died of bowel cancer, leaving behind a young wife and two teenage children. I had been his doctor for several months and by the time he died I thought I knew Fred and his family reasonably well. It was only after the eulogy and other tributes were completed that I realised how little I knew him after all. Not for the first time in my life, I was faced with two nagging questions. First, is it possible to really know someone, and if not, why not? Second, are we as mysterious to ourselves as we are to others?

Knowing what someone does, their likes and dislikes, their habits, hobbies, tastes, religion, cultural background, family and past history gives us information about their surface persona, but reveals little of what lies beneath. Conclusions drawn from interacting with another may be inaccurate for the character we get to know may, in the words of Paul Tournier be, 'the willing watchdog of the person' (1957, p.143). It guards the treasure that lies deep within and this treasure often remains unknown, not only to others but also to the person him/herself. The picture is further distorted because the observer sees only what they want to see and their vision is limited by their own persona. This is expressed beautifully in the following adage, 'We fail to see through the window because we paint pictures on the glass' (original source unknown). In palliative care, fear and anxiety contribute to the pictures on the glass dictating what is said and also what is heard. Emotions cloud understanding and compromise authenticity.

To overcome the blocks to authentic communication and to interact with the dying person at a deeper level requires us to be aware of how our own watchdog is operating. Awareness puts the watchdog on hold and allows us to better hear the other person and to sense the emotions that accompany their words. When someone is encouraged to talk about how they feel and is really heard and accepted, they may touch on previously unexplored territory. Being heard by someone who has dropped their protective layers allows them to be vulnerable too and there is no need of their watchdog. Then, they may get in touch with deep feelings and feel safe enough to share them. This increases awareness and helps bring a sense of liberation and peace. They begin to know more about themselves and the meaning of their life.

Ideally, we build the reflective process into our lives well before the eleventh hour. Many, however, leave it to life's final chapter when the desire to discover the mystery of 'who am I?' becomes compelling and urgent. It is then an important part of their dying journey if they are to find meaning and fulfilment. Diagnosis of a life-threatening illness and impending death impels us toward self-discovery. It is not an easy path. Thomas Moore describes it as being a quarter inch long and several miles deep (1992). I interpret this to mean that the mystery of who we are only deepens the more we look for answers. This is not to say that the search for meaning is pointless but only that it is full of mystery. To not ask 'who am I?' would be to ignore the most fundamental question about our existence. Paraphrasing Jacques Lacarriene, we would be suffocated by the deceptive coils of an outer life.

Sometimes the value in reviewing our life depends on having another person hear what we have to say. Jean-Paul Sartre, the great French philosopher of the last century, said, 'I can only know myself through the intermediary of another person.' To be present and listen while the dying person reflects upon their life, their achievements, their mistakes, the sadness and the joy, is a wonderful gift we can offer. A process that facilitates healing for the listened-to and the listener. It helps shed some of the 'deceptive coils that envelop the chrysalis.' Not only does the person speaking get a little closer to understanding the meaning of their life and who they really are, but the person listening also starts to see through the chrysalis. The mystery of 'who' is dying comes more into focus.

Dying presents all of us with the opportunity to grow, to change, to love, to appreciate and ultimately to glimpse the meaning of our existence. Our death is the completion of our life's mission. The sun as it sets may have lost much of its early brightness but this has unexpected rewards for it can, often for the first time, be clearly seen. Although it seems paradoxical, truth and the mystery of 'Who am I?' may be revealed in the final moments of our life.

When asked how he could create such beautiful sculptures from ordinary blocks of marble, Michelangelo said, 'The beauty lies within; all I do is remove the excesses'. Like Michelangelo's chisel, allowing someone to talk about their life may help remove some of the excesses and allow their essential nature to shine through.

Epilogue

One only fears what
one does not understand

ANTON CHEKOV

Death, and much of what happens around the time of death is a mystery. I, like many who work in palliative care, am challenged emotionally and spiritually by the experience of caring for people who are dying. Stories and experiences similar to those described throughout this book have helped formulate my beliefs about life and death, and how I can best be present for those at life's end. Although I have been doing this privileged work for twenty five years I am constantly learning and relearning, and there is much that I do not understand. We are all different and the obstacles people have to contend with as they approach death are unique to them and their way of life.

The purpose in writing this book is not to glamorise death or prove there is life after death but to underline the need for a more holistic approach to the care of the dying. Death is not the conclusion to a series of medical events, it is a profound human experience. As someone approaches death, their emotional and spiritual needs are as great if not greater than those of their bodies. If we attend only to the physical envelope, the soul suffers and the real significance of death is lost, as is the opportunity for sharing and healing. Deathbed visions and other near-to-death experiences are part of this healing experience. They are extraordinary gifts waiting to be shared and are often overlooked because we do not understand or appreciate their meaning or their significance.

The following story features many of these gifts and illustrates the healing potential that is available for those who are graced by them. Each of the experiences that is described draws attention to the profoundly symbolic message that permeate near-to-death phenomena and shows how some could easily be attributed to a hallucination or delirium. As has been stated and restated throughout the book it is not so much the words, but the implicit message that is important. Understanding these messages opens all to what is being revealed and to the mystery that surrounds death.

Aaron was the 37 year-old son of Greg and Anna, and brother to Matthew and Alana. In 2014 Aaron was found to have Stage 4 lymphoma. It was an extremely rare variant of lymphoma and failed to respond to the numerous attempts at cure. Throughout his illness, especially in those final weeks Anna sought to create a loving and harmonious space around her son and constantly prayed for divine assistance. She says, 'I began to pray as only a mother can for her dying child! I called on GOD and all the heavenly hosts that can assist my son make a safe transition into the LIGHT! I called on Archangel Michael to stand guard over Aaron, and use his powerful blue sword to cut away all negative or evil forces! I asked him to blaze his blue flame in & around my son and protect him for all eternity.'

Four days before Aaron died, Anna arrived at the hospital to find him in a state of panic. He felt there was something wrong with his brain, for there before him he could see a man sitting on a blue couch. He knew he could not possibly be there, but he was there! Anna thought Aaron must be hallucinating and told him so. Aaron accepted this, but minutes later he asked, "Who is the Hollywood guy standing next to the couch?" Anna had no answer. Later that day, Aaron turned to his mother and said, "Mum, I have something important to tell you; there's a giant blue plant in this room and it's HUGE." These were his last words. In the remaining days of Aaron's life Anna, Greg, his two siblings Matthew and Alana, her partner Brent and their little girl Ava Bliss remained by his side.

While all this was happening Anna's sister, Orissia, was holidaying some distance away. One night she had a dream in which a woman of 'Significant Authority', who she thought to be a Guardian of the Portal to the other side, gave her access to Aaron's great-grandfather (who incidentally had died ten years before Aaron's birth). She was overjoyed at seeing him and wanted to tell him everything about the family. He, however, stopped her abruptly and said he was there to talk about Aaron. He said he was waiting for Aaron. She then saw an image that she can only describe as his 'energy field' that spun like a tornado and took in Aaron's own energy field, lifting him upwards in a spiral motion. Orissia woke, and knowing this was an omen she made immediate plans to return to Melbourne. She arrived at the hospital and was there with Anna and Greg when Aaron died two hours later. As nurses and the pastoral care worker gathered around his bed, Anna and her family directed Aaron to soar like an eagle towards the light. Despite the enormous sadness felt by all, Anna was still able to say, "The love in that room touched everyone's heart."

We now jump ahead some six months to the time of Greg's cardiac arrest. He was in hospital at the time having been admitted for drainage of a large cyst on the left kidney. The code blue team was called and it took them just over 10 minutes to revive him. The next day, with tears streaming down his face, Greg told Anna he had seen Aaron. He was stunned by how beautiful he looked and described him as follows, "He had long golden hair, looked 20 years old, was wearing a radiant white shimmering robe and radiated brilliant light." He said there were a group of beings behind Aaron, but he couldn't distinguish who they were. A magnificent bridge separated Greg from Aaron and the other beings. Eager to embrace his son, Greg attempted to cross the bridge, but was stopped in his tracks when Aaron put his hand up and firmly repeated 3 times, "Dad stop, you must go back, it's not your time." Greg's last memory is watching them fade away.

Days later Greg was still trying to work out how he heard Aaron's voice reverberating inside his head. Although separated from Aaron by a large bridge he still heard Aaron's voice ordering him to go back. He insists, "It was, without doubt, Aaron's earthly voice." Greg also wonders about the two beings who were standing on either side of Aaron. They were slightly older and equally radiant and he now suspects they were instructing Aaron about what to say. Greg says the scenery was very ordinary where he was standing and was exquisite and vibrant where Aaron and the others stood. He describes magnificent but unidentifiable plants and says everything shimmered with radiant light. It was all "hyper-real."

After Aaron's death and prior to this experience Greg was, according to Anna, a broken man. He kept to himself and would often break down and sob uncontrollably. He made frequent trips to Aaron's grave and was often heard to say, "If only I could see my son once more." No amount of family support or counselling lessened his grief, yet it all evaporated dramatically after his near-death experience.

Anna concludes, "To say that Greg was happy and excited to see his son is a huge understatement."

This near-death experience has changed Greg's life as well as his perspective on life and death. He describes it as the most beautiful and profound experience he has ever had.

Bibliography

Achterberg J, Cooke K, Richards T, Standish L, Kozak L, Lake J. (2005). Evidence for correlation between Distant Intentionality and brain function in recipients. *Journal of Alternative and Complimentary Medicine*; 11(6): 965-971.

Ashby M. (2009) *The Study of Dying* Ed. A Kellehear. Cambridge Uni. Press: New York

Alexander E. (2012). *Proof of Heaven*. Simon & Schuster: New York.

Aurell J and Elmqvist D. (1985) Sleep in the surgical intensive care unit: Continuous polygraphic recording of sleep in nine patients receiving post-operative care. *British Medical Journal* 290: 1029–1032.

Austin JH. (2006) *Zen Brain Reflections*. MIT Press: Cambridge.

Auyong DB, Klein SM, Gan TJ, Roche AM, Olson DW, Habib AS. (2010) Processed electroencephalogram during donation after cardia death. *Anaesthesia-Analgesia*; 110(5): 1428-1432.

Bailey LW and Yates J (eds). (1996) *The Near-death Experience*. Routledge: New York.

Barbato M. (2001) Bispectral index monitoring in unconscious palliative care patients. *Journal of Palliative Care* 17.2: 102–108.

Barbato M, Blunden C, Reid K and Rodriguez P. (1999) Parapsychological phenomena near the time of death. *Journal of Palliative Care* 15.2: 30–37.

Barbato M. (2010) *Caring for the Living and the Dying*. Self-published: Sydney.

Barrett W. (1918) *On the Threshold of the Unseen*. Kegan Paul: London.

Barrett W. (1986; first published 1926) *Death-Bed Visions*. The Aquarian Press: Wellingborough.

Beirne P. (2002) *Crossing boundaries*. In Rumbold B. (ed) *Spirituality and Palliative Care*. Oxford University Press: Melbourne.

Berman P. (1996) *The Journey Home*. Pocket Books: New York.

Betty SL. (2006). Are they hallucinations or are they the spirituality of deathbed and near-death visions. *Omega*; 53(1-2); 37-49.

Blackman S. (1997) *Graceful Exits: How Great Beings Die.* Weatherhill Inc: New York.

Blackmore S. (1984) A postal survey of out-of-body experiences and other experiences *Journal of the Society of Psychical Research* 52: 227–244.

Blackmore S. (1991) Near-death experiences: In or out of the body. *Skeptical Inquirer* 16: 34–45.

Blackmore S. (1996) Near-death experiences. *Journal of the Royal Society of Medicine* 89: 73–76.

Blackmore S. (2001) What can the paranormal teach us about consciousness? *Skeptical Inquirer* 25(2): 22–27.

Blackmore S. (2003) *Consciousness; an introduction.* Hodder and Stoughton: Abingdon.

Blanke O, Mohr C, Michel C, Pascual-Leone A, Brugger P, Seeck Margitta, Landis T and Thut G. (2005) Linking out-of-body experiences and self-processing to mental own-body imagery at the tempero-parietal junction. *The Journal of Neuroscience* 25(3): 550–557

Borjigin J, Lee UC, Liu T, Pal D, Huff D et al. (2013) Surge of neurophysiological coherence and connectivity in the dying brain. *PNAS*; 110(35): 14432-14437.

Braden G. (2007) *The Divine Matrix – Bridging Time, Space, Miracles, and Belief.* Hay House: New York.

Brayne S, Lovelace H, Fenwick P. (2008). End-of-life experiences and the dying process in a Gloucestershire nursing home as reported by nurses and care assistants. *American Journal of Hospice and Palliative Care;* 25(3): 195-206.

Byock I. (2002) The meaning and value of death. *Journal of Palliative Care* 5(2): 279–288.

Callahan D. (1993) Pursuing a peaceful death. *Hastings Centre Report* 23(4): 33–38.

Chawla LS, Akst S, Junker C, Jacobs B, Seneff M. (2009). Surges of electrical activity at the time of death. *Journal of Palliative Medicine*; 12(12): 1095-1100.

Claxton G. (1994) *Noises from the Darkroom*. The Aquarian Press: London.

Cole R. (1999) *Mission of Love*. Lothian Books: Port Melbourne.

Currow DC, Burns CM and Abernethy AP. (2008) Place of death for people with non-cancer and cancer illness in South Australia: a population-based survey. *Journal of Palliative Care* 24(3): 144–150.

Dalai Lama. (2002) *The Dalai Lama in Dialogue: On the Science of the Mind*. Mind Science Forum. ANU: Canberra.

Datson SL and Marwit SJ. (1997) Personality constructs and perceived presence of deceased loved ones. *Death Studies* 21: 131–146.

Davidson J. (1995) *The Gospel of Jesus*. Element Books Ltd: Dorset.

Davies N and Quinn T. (2005) Opioid-related musical hallucinations. *The Lancet* 29(4): 327–328.

de Chardin T. (1968) *The Divine Milieu*. Harper and Row: New York.

Dharmawardena G. (1996) www.purifymind.com/WuantumMechnicalMod.htm

Diver S. (1999) *Survival*. Pan Macmillan: Sydney.

Doughty C. (2014) *Smoke Gets in Your Eyes*. W W Norton & Co.: New York

Ethier AM. (2005) Death-related sensory experiences. *Journal Paediatric Oncology Nursing* 22(2): 104–111.

Faraday A. (1974) *The Dream Game*. Harper and Row: New York.

Fenwick P and Fenwick E (2008). *The Art of Dying*. Continuum: London.

Finneran RJ (ed). (1996) *The*

Collected Poems of WB Yeats. Simon and Schuster: New York.

Fins JJ, Miller FG, Acres CA, Bacchetta MD and Huzzard LL. (1999) End-of-life decision making in the hospital: Current practice and future prospects. *Journal of Pain and Symptom Management* 17(1): 6–15.

Fox M. (2003) *Religion, spirituality and the near-death experience.* Routledge: London.

Fox M, Nijeboer S, Solomonova E, Domhoff GW and Christoff K. (2013) Dreaming as mind wandering. *Frontiers in Human Neuroscience* 7; Article 412: 1-17

French CC. (2005) Near-death experiences in cardiac arrest survivors. *Progress in Brain Research* 150: 351–367.

Gauntlett-Gilbert J and Kuipers E. (2003) Phenomenology of visual hallucinations in psychiatric conditions. *The Journal of Nervous and Mental Disease* 191(3): 203–208.

Grant P. (2014) The significance of end-of-life dreams and visions. *Nursing Times*; 110(28): 22-24.

Greyson B. (1983) The near-death experience scale. *The Journal of Nervous and Mental Disease* 171(8): 369–375.

Greyson B. (1993) Varieties of near-death experience. *Psychiatry* 56: 390–399.

Greyson B. (2000) Dissociation in people who have near-death experiences: out of their bodies or out of their minds? *The Lancet* 355: 460–463.

Greyson B and Bush NE. (1996) *Distressing near-death experiences*. In Bailey LW, Yates J (eds) *The Near-Death Experience*. Routledge: New York.

Greyson B and Stevenson MD. (1980) The phenomenology of near-death experience. *American Journal Psychiatry* 137(10): 1193–1196.

Griffiths B. (1980) *The Golden String.* Templegate Publishers: Illinois.

Grosso M. (1996) *The Archetype of Death and Enlightenment.* In Bailey LW, Yates J (eds) *The Near-Death Experience.* Routledge: New York.

Houran J and Lange R. (1997)

Hallucinations that comfort: contextual mediation of deathbed visions. *Perceptual and Motor Skills* 84: 1491–1504.

Humphrey N. (1992) *A History of the Mind.* Chatto Windus Ltd: London.

James W. (1985; first published 1902) *The Varieties of Religious Experience.* Penguin Classics: New York.

James W. (1995) *Pragmatism.* Dover Publications Inc: New York.

Jansen K. (1995) Using ketamine to induce the near-death experience: mechanism of action and therapeutic potential. *Yearbook for Ethnomedicine and Study of Consciousness* 4: 55–81.

Jones G. (1998) *Magnanimous Despair.* Boombana Publications: Mount Nebo.

Joseph R. (1992) *The Right Brain and the Unconscious.* Plenum Press: New York.

Joseph R. (2004) *The left and right hemisphere: The split-brain.* www.Brain-Mind.com

Jouvet M. (1999) *The Paradox of Sleep.* Bradford Books: London.

Judson IR and Wiltshaw E. (1983) A near-death experience. *Lancet* 3: 561–562.

Kalish RA and Reynolds DK. (1973) Phenomenological reality and post-death contact. *Journal for the Scientific Study of Religion*: 209–221.

Kavanaugh RE. (1974) *Facing Death.* Penguin: Baltimore.

Kearney M. (1996). *Mortally Wounded.* Marino: Dublin.

Kearney M. (2000) *A Place of Healing.* Oxford University: Oxford Press.

Kellehear A (ed). (2000) *Death and Dying in Australia.* Oxford University Press: Melbourne.

Kellehear A. (2007) *A Social History of Dying.* Cambridge University Press: Melbourne.

Kennedy JE and Kanthamani H. (1995). An exploratory study of the effects of paranormal and spiritual experiences on peoples' lives and well-being. *The Journal of the American Society for Psychical Research*; 89: 249–264.

Kerr CW, Donnelly JP, Wright ST, Kuszczak SM, Banas A, Grant P, Luczkiewicz DL. (2014). End-of-life dreams and visions. *Journal of Palliative Medicine*; 17(3): 296-303.

Kessler D. (1997) *The Rights of the Dying*. Vermillion: London.

Koestenbaum P. (1976) *Is There an Answer to Death?* Prentice-Hall Inc: New Jersey.

Komp D. (1992) *A Window to Heaven*. Zondervan Publishing: Michigan.

Kübler-Ross E. (1991) *On Life after Death*. Celestial Arts: California.

Lawrence M. (1995) The unconscious experience. *American Journal of Critical Care* 4: 227–232.

Lawrence M. (1997) *In a World of their Own*. Bergin and Garvey: Connecticut.

Lawrence M and Repede E. (2012). The incidence of deathbed communications and their impact on the dying process. *American Journal of Hospice and Palliative Care*; 30(7): 632-639.

Lorimer D. (1990) *Whole in One*. Penguin: London.

MacLeod AD. (2009) Lightening up Before Death. *Journal of Supportive and Palliative Care*; 7: 513-516

Martin GD. (1990) *Shadows in the Cave*. Arkana: London.

Merikle P. (1998) Psychological investigations of unconscious perception. *Journal of Conscious Studies* 5(1): 5–18.

Middlewood S, Gardner G and Gardner A. (2001) Dying in hospital: medical failure or natural outcome. *Journal of Pain and Symptom Management* 22(6): 1035–41.

Miller J. (2001). *The Art of Being a Healing Presence*. Willowgreen: Indiana.

Moody RA. (1975). *Life after Life*. Bantam: New York.

Moore T. (1992). *Care of the Soul*. HarperCollins: New York.

Moorjani A (2012). *Dying To Be Me*. Hay House: London

Morse M. (1994) Near-death experiences and death related visions in children: implications for the clinician. *Current Problems in Paediatrics* 24: 55–83.

Morse M. (1995) *Parting Visions*. Judy Piatkus Publishers Ltd: London.

Morse M, Castillo P, Venecia D, Milstein J and Tyler D.

(1986) Childhood near-death experiences. *American Journal of Diseases in Chidhood* 140: 1110–1114.

Murphy M. (1999) *The Wisdom of Dying*. Element Books Ltd: Dorset.

Nadeau R. and Kafatos M. (1999) *The Non-local Universe: The New Physics and Matters of the Mind.* Oxford University Press: New York.

Nayani TH and David AS. (1996) The auditory hallucination: a phenomenological survey. *Psychological Medicine* 26:177–189.

Nelson P. (1994) *There's a Hole in my Sidewalk: The Romance of Self-discovery*. Beyond Words Publishing Company: Hillsboro.

O'Connor D. (2003) Palliative care nurses' experience of paranormal phenomena and their influence on nursing practice *Making Sense of Dying and Death Inter-disciplinary Conference* Paris.

Osho. (2001) *Intuition – Knowing Beyond Logic*. St Martin's Press: New York.

Osis K and Haraldsson E. (1977) *At the Hour of our Death*. Hastings House: Connecticut.

Parnia S and Fenwick P. (2001) Near-death experiences in cardiac arrest: visions of a dying brain or visions of a new science of consciousness. *Resuscitation* 52: 5–11.

Parnia S, Waller DG, Yeates R and Fenwick P. (2002) A qualitative and quantitative study of the incidence, features and aetiology of near-death experiences in cardiac arrest survivors. *Resuscitation* 48: 149–156.

Paver J. (2002) *Supervision and palliative care for the care-givers*. In Rumbold B (ed) *Spirituality and Palliative Care*. Oxford University Press: Melbourne.

Penfield W. (1975) *The Mystery of the Mind: A critical study of consciousness and the human brain.* Princeton University Press: Princeton.

Persinger M. (1983) Religious and mystical experiences as artefacts of temporal lobe function: a general hypothesis. *Perceptual and Motor Skills* 57: 1255–1262.

Persinger M. (1999) *Neuropsychological Bases of God Beliefs*. Praeger: Westport.

Rawlings M. (1980) *Before Death Comes*. Nelson: Nashville.

Reanney D. (1991) *The Death of Forever*. Longman Cheshire: Melbourne.

Rees WD. (1971) The hallucinations of widowhood. *British Medical Journal* 4: 37–41.

Rinbochay L and Hopkins J. (1979) *Death, Intermediate State and Rebirth in Tibetan Buddhism*. Rider: London.

Ring K. (1980) *Life at Death*. Coward, McCann and Geoghegan: New York.

Ring K. (1984) *Heading Towards Omega – in Search of the Meaning of the Near-Death Experience*. Quill: New York.

Rinpoche S. (1992) *The Tibetan Book of Living and Dying*. Random House: London.

Roberts G and Owen J. (1988) The near-death experience. *British Journal of Psychiatry* 153: 607–617.

Ross CA and Joshi S. (1992) Paranormal experiences in the general population. *The Journal of Nervous and Mental Disease* 180(6): 357–361.

Sanders MA. (2007) *Nearing Death Awareness*. Jessica Kingsley Publishers: London.

Schooler JW, Smallwood J, Christoff K, Handy TC, Reichle ED and Sayette MA. (2011). Meta-awareness, perceptual decoupling and the wandering mind. *Trends in Cognitive Sciences* 15(7): 319-326

Shapiro CM and Flanigan MJ. (1993) Function of sleep. *British Medical Journal* 306: 383–385.

Sheldrake R. (2005) *Morphic fields and morphic resonance*; an introduction. http://www.sheldrake.org

Shestov L. (1975) *In Job's Balances: on the Sources of the Eternal Truths*, trans, Coventry C and Macartney CA. Ohio University Press: Ohio.

Siegel RK. (1980) The psychology of life after death. *American Psychologist* 35(10): 911–931.

Stevenson I. (1983) Do we need a new word to supplement "hallucination"? *Am. J Psychiatry* 140: 1609–1611.

Stokes M, Voytek B. http://www.nature.com/scitable/blog/brain-metrics/could_a_final_surge_in (downloaded 19/8/15)

Teunisse RJ, Cruysberg JR, Hoefnagels WH, Verbeek AL and Zitman FG. (1996) Visual hallucinations in psychologically normal people: Charles Bonnet's syndrome. *Lancet* 347: 794–797.

The Sunday Mail. (October 8, 2006): Brisbane.

Thoreau H. (2004; first published 1854)) *Walden*. Collectors Library: London.

Tournier P. (1957) *The Meaning of Persons* London: SCH Press.

van Lommel P, van Wees R, Meyers V and Elfferich I. (2001) Near-death experience in survivors of cardiac arrest: a prospective study in the Netherlands *Lancet* 358: 2039–2045.

Van Lommel P. (2004) About the continuity of our consciousness. *Advances in Experimental Biology* 550: 115–132.

Whinnery JE. (1990) Acceleration-induced loss of consciousness. *Arch Neurol* 47: 764–776.

Wilber K. (1977) *Spectrum of Consciousness*. Wheaton Illanois: Quest.

Wilber K. (1983) *Eye to Eye*. Shambhala Publications: Boston, Massachusetts.

Wilber K and Wilber T. (2001) *Grace and Grit*. Gateway: Dublin.

Wills-Brandon C. (2000) *One Last Hug Before I Go*. Health, Communications Inc: Deerfield Beach.

Yogananda P. (1995) *The Bhagavad Gita*. Self-Realisation Fellowship: Los Angeles.